My Dearest, Dearest Albert

My Dearest, Dearest Albert

Queen Victoria's Life Through Her Letters and Journals

Compiled by Karen Dolby

Michael O'Mara Books Limited

First published in Great Britain in 2018 by
Michael O'Mara Books Limited
9 Lion Yard
Tremadoc Road
London SW4 7NQ

A CIP catalogue record for this book is available from the British Library.

Papers used by Michael O'Mara Books Limited are natural,
recyclable products made from wood grown in sustainable forests.
The manufacturing processes conform to the environmental
regulations of the country of origin.

ISBN: 978-1-78243-967-7 in hardback print format
ISBN: 978-1-78243-971-4 in ebook format

1 2 3 4 5 6 7 8 9 10

Designed and typeset by Ed Pickford

Printed and bound by CPI Group (UK) Ltd, Croydon, CR0 4YY

www.mombooks.com

Contents

❧ Introduction ❧

'I must conclude, my dearest, beloved Albert. Be careful as to your valuable health, and be assured that no one loves you as much as your faithful Victoria.'

30 December 1839

Victoria put pen to paper every day, and kept a diary from the age of thirteen; she was also an enthusiastic letter writer throughout her life. Few have written as prolifically or as openly, particularly no monarch as iconic as Queen Victoria, whose reign would last more than sixty-three years.

Official correspondence offers a glimpse of Victoria's opinions, but her true character springs from the pages of her journals and private letters. Those sent to her eldest daughter Vicky, whom she considered 'more as if it were my sister', and to her Uncle Leopold are especially intimate. Letters to Leopold I, her maternal uncle and the King of the Belgians, were originally written as a duty but the two would develop a close and loving bond. Her missives and diary entries span the decades of the Queen's long life and create a revealing portrait of Victoria as monarch, wife and mother. They reference her interests,

I

views and ideas on all manner of subjects, from the role of women in society to the books she enjoyed reading, as well as gossip and insights into her sometimes complex relationships with her children. Underpinning it all is her absolute adoration of her beloved husband, her dearest, dearest Albert.

The young princess opens her first diary with the words: 'This book, Mamma gave me, that I might write the journal of my journey to Wales in it.' Her mother inspected the entries each evening until Victoria became Queen in June 1837, aged eighteen, and firmly asserted her independence.

She was to fill 122 volumes of journals during the course of her life, as well as writing daily letters. It has been estimated that Victoria wrote over two thousand words a day, which amounts to a staggering sixty million words over her lifetime. She stopped writing just ten days before her death. In line with the Queen's instructions, her youngest daughter Beatrice later edited the journals, removing anything she considered too personal or that might offend the royal family. Beatrice transcribed the contents, cutting them to 111 volumes and subsequently destroyed the originals, much to the horror of Victoria's grandson King George V and his wife Queen Mary. Unbeknown to Beatrice, Lord Esher had made a typescript of the earlier volumes for his book *The Girlhood of Queen Victoria: A Selection From Her Majesty's Diaries Between the Years 1832 and 1840*. The surviving journals and letters, illustrated with Victoria's own sketches and watercolours, are stored in the Royal Archives at Windsor Castle and from 2012 were made available online.

Victoria writes openly and in great detail, showing herself to be emotional and honest about her own feelings and experiences, as well as her opinions of other people. She praises her husband Albert endlessly and pours out her love and desire for him as her adored lover, friend and companion. The entries chronicling her devastation at his early death are heartbreakingly sad.

Photographs of Queen Victoria most commonly show a plump figure, serious and regal, dressed in widow's black. The posed portraits of the day were stiff, formal affairs, mainly because their subjects had to stay still so long for the image to develop. In reality, the personality of Alexandrina Victoria, Queen of the United Kingdom of Great Britain and Ireland, and later Empress of India, is rather different. In private, at least, Victoria had a reputation for being fun-loving and entertaining. Like her great-great-granddaughter Queen Elizabeth II, she became Queen at a young age and preferred to maintain a composed and dignified appearance in public, perhaps to add gravitas to her youth. In a similar way to Elizabeth II, she also fell in love with her husband during one of their first meetings.

Today, the idea of Victorian values suggests restraint and infers a rather old-fashioned and strict code of conduct. In fact, the Victorian era was one of development and innovation, introducing a speed of change never before seen that affected and transformed every aspect of society. And at the forefront was Victoria – the first monarch to ride on a steam train, to have electricity installed at Buckingham Palace, and to witness the first-ever public demonstration of a telephone.

This book reveals the more human face of Victoria, from spirited young Queen to passionate bride and caring mother, and is told through her own words using selected passages from her journals and more personal letters.

Her writings are peppered with underlinings and capital letters, which add emphasis in her handwritten originals but look odd on the printed page. For ease of reading they are not included here and the words that she abbreviates are mostly written in full.

Victoria and Albert: a Passionate Partnership

Victoria and Albert: a Passionate Partnership

In 1839, just two years into her reign, the twenty-year-old Queen was somewhat resistant to the idea of marriage, for she was enjoying her newly found freedom and sense of authority far too much. She was also a romantic and wanted to marry for love, although she was very aware of her duty to choose the right partner as consort.

Throughout her adolescence, Victoria had been presented with a string of possible suitors, none of whom really found favour in her critical eyes. As the female heir to the British throne, the young Princess knew she was an attractive dynastic proposition for the sons of the aristocracy at home, as well as the royal families across Europe, but as Queen she was in no immediate hurry to choose a husband.

Royal Suitors

Her maternal uncle and adviser, Leopold I of Belgium, was keen on an alliance with his nephew Albert of Saxe-Coburg and Gotha. Leopold was brother to both Victoria's mother, Victoria, the Duchess of Kent, and Albert's father, Ernest I

Duke of Saxe-Coburg and Gotha, and Albert had been introduced to Victoria in May 1836 when she was almost seventeen. At that time, she was rather unimpressed with her cousin, Albert, and viewed him as too reserved. He was prone to fainting fits, preferred quiet evenings to the dances of which Victoria was so fond and seemed dull to the lively young Princess. He failed to cut a very romantic figure and, more importantly, marriage was not high on Victoria's list of priorities at that point.

Not easily dissuaded, Leopold decided that all Albert needed was a little coaching. He appointed Baron Christian Friedrich von Stockmar to tutor Albert for a future role as the Queen's consort. As well as providing invaluable counsel to the Prince, Stockmar was also a regular visitor to the British court, his name appearing with increasing frequency in Victoria's journals. On 20 June 1837, the day of her accession, she noted that while she was eating breakfast, 'good, faithful Stockmar came and talked to me'.

In her journal for April 1839, Victoria recorded a conversation with her Prime Minister, Lord Melbourne, on the subject of her marriage:

> Well, I mustered up courage, and said that my Uncle's great wish – was – that I should marry my Cousin Albert – who was with Stockmar … then he said, 'Cousins are not very good things,' and 'Those Coburgs are not popular abroad; the Russians hate them.' I then

said, who was there else? We enumerated the various Princes, of whom not one, I said, would do. For myself, I said, at present *my* feeling was quite against ever marrying … He said, 'It's a very serious thing, both as it concerns the Political effect and your own happiness.'

By the summer of 1839, Leopold decided his nephew was sufficiently tutored and ready for another meeting with the young Queen. Victoria remained reluctant, however, and in her journal of 12 July her thoughts on the match are very clear: 'Talked of my Cousins Ernest and Albert coming over – my having no great wish to see Albert, as the whole subject was an odious one …'

Nevertheless, on 15 July, she wrote to her uncle in the most diplomatic terms:

Though all the reports of Albert are most favourable, and though I have little doubt I shall like him, still one can never answer beforehand for feelings, and I may not have the feeling for him which is requisite to ensure happiness. I may like him as a friend, and as a cousin and as a brother, but no more.

Albert took offence at Victoria's lack of enthusiasm and was not easily persuaded to agree to visit the British court again. Having herself written to Uncle Leopold on 25 September to delay the arrival of her cousins by a few days because 'a number of the Ministers are coming down here on Monday to stay till Thursday, on affairs of great importance' the Queen was not at all impressed when Albert and Ernest further postponed their visit. She wrote to her Uncle Leopold on 1 October 1839 complaining of their apparent reluctance:

> … The retard of these young people puts me rather out, but of course cannot be helped. I had a letter from Albert yesterday saying they could not set off, he thought before the 6th. I think they don't exhibit much *empressement* [eagerness] to come here, which rather shocks me.

The Queen in Love

Any reservations Victoria may have felt about Albert were swept away when the couple finally met again in October 1839 at Windsor Castle. Upon seeing him for the first time in almost three-and-a-half years, the young Queen was amazed at the transformation. She was impressed by his character and morals, and her diary revealed that she found the young Prince 'so handsome and pleasing', adding, 'but the charm of his countenance is his expression, which is most delightful'.

When they danced together on 11 October, Victoria gave Albert a flower from her bouquet. Dressed in uniform that lacked a buttonhole, Albert cut a small hole in his jacket and placed the flower over his heart. The Queen was enchanted and her journal entry for the day clearly conveys her infatuation:

> Albert really is quite charming, and so excessively handsome, such beautiful blue eyes, an exquisite nose, and such a pretty mouth with delicate moustachios and very slight whiskers; a beautiful figure, broad in the shoulders and a fine waist; my heart is quite going … It is quite a pleasure to look at Albert when he gallops and valses, he does it so beautifully, holds himself so well with that beautiful figure of his.

She summarized the first couple of days spent with Albert and Ernest in an enthusiastic letter to her Uncle Leopold on 12 October 1839:

> The dear cousins arrived at half-past seven on Thursday, after a very bad and almost dangerous passage … Ernest is grown quite handsome; Albert's beauty is most striking, and he so amiable and unaffected – in short, very fascinating; he is excessively admired here … We rode out yesterday and danced after dinner. The young men are very amiable, delightful companions, and I am very happy to have them here; they are playing some Symphonies of Haydn under me at this very moment; they are passionately fond of music.

A mere five days after Albert's arrival in England, Victoria had no doubts about their mutual attraction and affection. As royal tradition dictated that no one could propose to a reigning monarch, Victoria asked Albert to marry her on 15 October 1839. The momentous occasion was duly recorded in her journal:

> At about ½ p.12, I sent for Albert … He came to the Closet where I was alone, and after a few minutes I said to him, that I thought he must be aware why I wished him to come here – and that it would make me too happy if he would consent to what I wished (to marry me); we embraced each other over and over again, and he was so kind, so affectionate … I really felt it was the happiest brightest moment in my life.

She wrote to her Uncle Leopold later the same day to give him the news and disclose her desire to marry Albert as swiftly as possible:

> My dearest Uncle – This letter will, I am sure, give you pleasure, for you have always shown and taken so warm an interest in all that concerns me. My mind is quite made up – and I told Albert this morning of it; the warm affection he showed me on learning this gave me great pleasure. He seems perfection, and I think that I have the prospect of very great happiness before me. I love him more than I can say, and I shall do everything in my

power to render the sacrifice he has made (for a sacrifice in my opinion it is) as small as I can. He seems to have a very great tact – a very necessary thing in his position. These last few days have passed like a dream to me, and I am so much bewildered by it all that I know hardly how to write; but I do feel very, very happy.

It is absolutely necessary that this determination of mine should be known to no one but yourself, and Uncle Ernest [Albert's father] – till the meeting of Parliament … Lord Melbourne, whom I of course have consulted about the whole affair, quite approves my choice, and expresses great satisfaction at the event, which he thinks in every way highly desirable. Lord Melbourne has acted in this business, as he has always done towards me, with the greatest kindness and affection.

We also think it better, and Albert quite approves of it, that we should be married very soon after Parliament meets, about the beginning of February; and indeed, loving Albert as I do, I cannot wish it should be delayed. My feelings are a little changed, I must say, since last Spring, when I said I couldn't think of marrying for three or four years; but seeing Albert has changed all this.

Writing in her journal on 1 November 1838, Victoria left no doubt as to the warmth of their feelings for each other:

Dearest Albert took my face in both his hands and kissed me most tenderly and said, *'ich habe dich so lieb, ich kann nicht sagen wie!*' ['I love you so much, I can't say how much!'] Dearest Angel, so kind of him, and he said we should be 'so *glucklich*' [happy] if I can only make him happy.

Her diary notes continued on the joys of being in love:

Oh! how blessed, how happy I am to think he is really mine; I can scarcely believe myself so blessed. I kissed his dear hand, and do feel so grateful to him; he is such an angel … We sit so nicely side by side on that little blue sofa; no two Lovers could ever be happier than we are!

The couple spent every possible moment together until Albert returned to Gotha in Germany on 14 November. Victoria's journal describes his departure and her feelings at his absence:

We kissed each other so often, and I leant on that dear soft cheek, fresh and pink like a rose … I gave Albert a last kiss, and saw him get into the carriage and – drive off. I cried much, felt wretched, yet happy to think that we should meet again so soon! Oh! how I love him, how intensely, how devotedly, how ardently! I cried and felt so sad. Wrote my journal. Walked. Cried.

A Royal Match

A great deal of diplomatic manoeuvring and brokering then followed before the marriage could go ahead. There was a heated debate in Parliament over the level of income that Albert should be granted and his precedence in terms of rank. There were also objections to his proposed naturalization as British. Victoria had initially wanted to make him King Consort, but had been persuaded by Lord Melbourne that this would not be a wise move. There was a great deal of anti-German sentiment amongst the public, especially as Albert came from a relatively unimportant state. Parliament was also initially keen to ensure the Prince had no political sway.

The details of the role that Albert would play, as well as matters concerning his household and expenses, were all areas of dispute. This may have been a love match but it was also a dynastic alliance and negotiations were not entirely straightforward. Albert was politically ambitious, although he lacked wealth and was the younger son of a minor German Duke.

On 28 November 1839, Victoria wrote to her future husband in response to his recent correspondence:

> This morning I received your dear, dear letter of the
> 21st. How happy do you make me with your love! Oh!
> my Angel Albert, I am quite enchanted with it! I do not
> deserve such love! Never, never did I think I could be
> loved so much.

Though Victoria loved her new fiancé deeply, as Queen she had no intention of conceding any power to him. Despite Albert's intention to choose the members of his own household, he was informed by Victoria that the British Establishment would not allow him to bring a German secretary or companion with him and he must instead accept Lord Melbourne's former private secretary George Anson.

Albert's response to the news revealed he was clearly upset:

> Think of my position. I am leaving my home with all its old
> associations, all my bosom friends and going to a country
> in which everything is strange to me – men, language,
> customs, modes of life. I have no one to confide in … Is
> it not to be conceded that the two or three persons who
> are to have the charge of my private affairs should be
> persons who already command my confidence?

But Victoria remained unmoved and was firm in her written reply, underlining almost every word for emphasis:

It is, as you rightly suppose, my greatest, my most anxious wish to do everything most agreeable to you, but I must differ with you respecting Mr Anson … What I said about Anson giving you advice, means, that if you like to ask him, he can and will be of the greatest use to you, as he is a very well-informed person … I am distressed to tell you what I fear you do not like, but it is necessary, my dearest, most excellent Albert. Once more I tell you that you can perfectly rely on me in these matters.

The question of Albert's private secretary continued to rankle and in her journal of 10 January 1840, Victoria referred to a conversation she had had with Lord Melbourne:

Talked of Albert's not quite understanding about his Household, which however, I said, I should make him easily understand. 'Don't let any difficulty stand in the way about George Anson,' said Lord M. kindly, but I said G. Anson was the fit person and that I should easily make him understand it.

In a letter to Albert written in January 1840, Victoria explained the official ruling over heraldic arms for her fiancé as a foreign Prince and how the matter would be resolved:

Now as to the Arms: as an English Prince you have no right, and Uncle Leopold had no right to quarter the English Arms, but the Sovereign has the power to allow it by Royal Command: this was done for Uncle Leopold by the Prince Regent, and I will do it again for you. But it can only be done by Royal Command. I will, therefore, without delay, have a seal engraved for you.

The pair also disagreed over the length of the honeymoon. Shortly before their wedding, on 31 January 1840, Victoria wrote to Albert from Buckingham Palace explaining her position very clearly:

… You have written to me in one of your letters about our stay at Windsor, but, dear Albert, you have not at all understood the matter. You forget, my dearest Love, that I am the Sovereign, and that business can stop and wait for nothing. Parliament is sitting, and something occurs almost every day, for which I may be required, and it is quite impossible for me to be absent from London; therefore two or three days is already a long time to be absent. I am never easy a moment, if I am not on the spot, and see and hear what is going on.

Albert would later comment that he was 'only the husband, not the master in my house'.

After considerable wrangling back and forth, matters were eventually resolved satisfactorily. Albert was escorted back to London in February 1840 as the final wedding preparations were made. Whatever diplomatic manoeuvring and politics lay behind the royal couple's marriage, there is no doubt that Victoria's passion for Albert was entirely reciprocated. Nevertheless, he was daunted by his role and saw a future 'strewn with thorns'. He was also not a popular choice with members of the British public, who largely viewed him as too German, humourless and intellectual.

Throughout the official negotiations, Victoria and Albert had continued their more personal correspondence. In November 1839, Albert expressed his innermost feelings in a letter to Victoria:

> Dearest deeply loved Victoria. I need not tell you that since we left, all my thoughts have been with you at Windsor, and that your image fills my whole soul. Even in my dreams I never imagined that I should find so much love on earth. How that moment shines for me still when I was close to you, with your hand in mine. Those days flew by so quickly, but our separation will

fly equally so … With promises of unchanging love and devotion, Your ever true Albert.

On 7 February 1840, Victoria noted in her journal that she had received 'a delightful letter from dearest Albert from Brussels dated the 4th, with a very funny book of Caricatures'. The next day she recorded that yet more correspondence had arrived:

> Just before I went out I received a delightful letter from dearest Albert from Dover, written in the morning; he suffered most dreadfully coming over; he is much pleased with the very kind reception he met with at Dover …
>
> At this moment I received a letter, and a dear one, from dearest Albert from Canterbury, where he had just arrived, and where he had also been very well received.

In the same diary entry she recorded in detail a conversation with Lord Melbourne. As well as being the first Prime Minister of her reign, Melbourne was her adviser and trusted friend. There is no doubt the pair had a close bond and felt genuine affection for one another:

> We were seated as usual, Lord Melbourne sitting near me. Talked of Bull-dogs; of the Marriage Ceremony; my being a little agitated and nervous; 'Most natural,' Lord M. replied warmly; 'how could it be otherwise?' Lord M.

was so warm, so kind, and so affectionate, the whole evening, and so much touched in speaking of me and my affairs. Talked of my former resolution of never marrying. 'Depend upon it, it's right to marry,' he said earnestly; 'if ever there was a situation that formed an exception, it was yours; it's in human nature, it's natural to marry; the other is a very unnatural state of things; it's a great change – it has its inconveniences; everybody does their best, and depend upon it you've done well; difficulties may arise from it,' as they do of course from everything. Talked of popular assemblies, of my having grown so thin … of the Addresses and dinners A. would be plagued with; of my taking him to the Play soon. 'There'll be an immense flow of popularity now,' Lord M. said. Talked of the difficulty of keeping quite free from all Politics. I begged Lord M. much to manage about Thursday [Victoria had invited Melbourne to stay at Windsor], which he promised he would, as I said it always made me so happy to have him. 'I am sure none of your friends are so fond of you as I am,' I said. 'I believe not,' he replied, quite touched, and I added also he had been always so very kind to me I couldn't say how I felt it.

On 8 February 1840, Albert arrived back at Buckingham Palace. Victoria's journal entry describes her joy at their reunion:

1st stepped out Ernest, then Uncle Ernest, and then Albert, looking beautiful and so well; I embraced him and took him by the hand and led him up to my room; Mamma, Uncle Ernest, and Ernest following … After dinner … I sat on the sofa with my beloved Albert, Lord Melbourne sitting near me. Lord M. admired the diamond Garter which Albert had on … I told him it was my gift; I also gave him (all before dinner) a diamond star I had worn, and badge.

A Royal Wedding

Victoria sent a hand-delivered note to Albert on the morning of their wedding. It was 10 February 1840 and the day was cold, wet and windy:

> Dearest – How are you to-day, and have you slept well?
> I have rested very well, and feel very comfortable to-day.
> What weather! I believe, however, the rain will cease.
> Send one word when you, my most dearly loved bridegroom, will be ready.
> Thy ever-faithful,
>
> Victoria R

Victoria and Albert were married at one o'clock in the Chapel Royal of St James's Palace, London, the first marriage of a reigning queen since Mary I to Philip II of Spain almost three hundred years earlier. It also marked a break with the tradition of royal marriages being solemnized at night.

At the time it was more usual for brides to wear coloured wedding dresses, woven with gold or silver. Instead, Victoria opted for a white satin dress made from silk spun in Spitalfields, east London, and instead of a crown or tiara she chose a simple headdress of orange blossoms, a symbol of fertility. She also carried a wreath made from the same flowers.

The Queen recorded everything about the day in her diary:

At ½ p.12 I set off, dearest Albert having gone before. I wore a white satin gown with a very deep flounce of Honiton lace, imitation of old. I wore my Turkish diamond necklace and earrings, and Albert's beautiful sapphire brooch [Albert was interested in jewellery and had it made specially for his bride]. Mamma and the Duchess of Sutherland went in the carriage with me. I never saw such crowds of people as there were in the Park, and they cheered most enthusiastically. When I arrived at St James's, I went into the dressing-room where my 12 young Train-bearers were, dressed all in white with white roses, which had a beautiful effect. Here I waited till dearest Albert's Procession had moved into the Chapel …

… The Ceremony was very imposing, and fine
and simple, and I think ought to make an everlasting
impression on every one who promises at the Altar
to keep what he or she promises. Dearest Albert repeated
everything very distinctly. I felt so happy when the ring
was put on, and by my precious Albert. As soon as the
Service was over, the Procession returned as it came, with
the exception that my beloved Albert led me out. The
applause was very great, in the Colour Court [one of a
number of courtyards at St James's Palace] as we came
through; Lord Melbourne, good man, was very much
affected during the Ceremony and at the applause.

After the ceremony Victoria was surprised at the public's
response, later committing her thoughts to paper:

I then returned to Buckingham Palace alone with Albert;
they cheered us really most warmly and heartily; the
crowd was immense; and the Hall at Buckingham Palace
was full of people; they cheered us again and again.

Looking back on the event she called it, 'The happiest day
of my life.'

The wedding breakfast was held at Buckingham Palace
and the elaborate cake weighed a staggering 300 pounds.
At four in the afternoon, dressed in a white silk gown
trimmed with swansdown and a bonnet with orange

flowers, Victoria left with Albert for their three-day
honeymoon at Windsor Castle.

Victoria described their wedding evening and night
candidly in her journal:

> We had our dinner in our sitting room; but I had such
> a sick headache that I could eat nothing, and was
> obliged to lie down in the middle blue room for the
> remainder of the evening on the sofa; but, ill or not,
> I never, never spent such an evening!! My dearest
> dearest dear Albert sat on a footstool by my side, and
> his excessive love and affection gave me feelings of
> heavenly love and happiness, I never could have hoped
> to have felt before! He clasped me in his arms, and
> we kissed each other again and again! His beauty, his
> sweetness and gentleness – really, how can I ever be
> thankful enough to have such a Husband! At ½ p.10
> I went and undressed and was very sick, and at 20
> m.p.10 we both went to bed; (of course in one bed), to
> lie by his side, and in his arms, and on his dear bosom,
> and be called by names of tenderness, I have never yet
> heard used to me before – was bliss beyond belief!
> Oh! This was the happiest day of my life! May God
> help me to do my duty as I ought and be worthy of
> such blessings.

She concluded the story of their first night together without a hint of Victorian modesty or prudishness:

> When day dawned (for we did not sleep much) and I
> beheld that beautiful face by my side, it was more than
> I can express! He does look so beautiful in his shirt only,
> with his beautiful throat seen.

The next day, in the grounds of Windsor Castle, the Queen recorded how she 'walked out with my precious Angel, all alone – so delightful, on the Terrace and new Walk, arm in arm', with 'Eos [Albert's greyhound] our only companion'.

During her honeymoon, the new bride wrote an ecstatic letter to her Uncle Leopold:

> My dearest Uncle – I write to you from here, the
> happiest, happiest Being that ever existed. Really, I
> do not think it possible for any one in the world to be
> happier, or as happy as I am. He is an Angel, and his
> kindness and affection for me is really touching. To look
> in those dear eyes, and that sunny face, is enough to
> make me adore him. What I can do to make him happy
> will be my greatest delight. Independent of my great
> personal happiness, the reception we both met with
> yesterday was the most gratifying and enthusiastic I ever
> experienced; there was no end of the crowds in London,

and all along the road. I was a good deal tired last night, but am quite well again to-day, and happy.

Unfortunately, it was the groom's turn to feel unwell and Victoria noted that 'Poor dear Albert felt sick and uncomfortable, and lay down in my room, while I wrote to Uncle Leopold ... He looked so dear, lying there and dozing.'

Forty-eight hours after their wedding and the bride was just as besotted:

> Already the 2nd day since our marriage; his love and gentleness is beyond everything, and to kiss that dear soft cheek, to press my lips to his, is heavenly bliss. I feel a purer more unearthly feel than I ever did. Oh! was ever woman so blessed as I am.

And the following morning she wrote: 'My dearest Albert put on my stockings for me. I went in and saw him shave; a great delight for me.' Interestingly, this is one of the entries that does not appear in Beatrice's edited journals but remains in Lord Esher's typed version of Victoria's original.

Although the couple sometimes had blazing arguments over the course of their passionate and tempestuous marriage, Victoria idolized Albert, describing him in one of her journal entries as 'perfection in every way ... Oh! how I adore and love him'.

In February 1861, Victoria wrote to her Uncle Leopold two days after what was to be their final wedding anniversary:

> On Sunday we celebrated, with feelings of deep gratitude and love, the twenty-first anniversary of our blessed marriage, a day which had brought us, and I may say the world at large, such incalculable blessings! Very few can say with me that their husband at the end of twenty-one years is not only full of the friendship, kindness and affection which a truly happy marriage brings with it, but the same tender love of the very first days of our marriage!

Victoria as Wife and Mother

Victoria as Wife and Mother

Writing later in life, Victoria looked back on her own childhood. She had been very isolated and lonely, especially after her half-sister married. Victoria had two half siblings, Carl and Feodora, from her mother's first marriage to Emich Carl, Prince of Leiningen, and although Feodora was almost twelve years older, the two sisters developed a close bond. The young Princess Victoria was not allowed to mix with other children: 'I had led a very unhappy life as a child – had no scope for my very violent feelings of affection ... and did not know what a happy domestic life was.'

Albert's early childhood had also been dysfunctional. His father, Ernest I, Duke of Saxe-Coburg and Gotha, was a famous philanderer who paid little attention to his younger son. His parents' turbulent marriage ended in divorce and his mother, Princess Louise of Saxe-Gotha-Altenburg, was exiled from court in 1824 when Albert was just five years old. She died seven years later without ever seeing her children again.

In contrast to their own experiences, Victoria and Albert wanted to be perfect parents and create the ideal family. From the outset, Albert saw his role as protecting and nurturing the British monarchy at a time when revolution threatened the royal families of Europe. Key to this were his efforts to modernize the royal family and present it as supremely loving, respectable and close-knit. The publicity worked and Victoria wrote delightedly, 'They say no Sovereign was ever more loved than I (I am bold enough to say), and this because of our happy domestic home and the good example it presents.'

The couple's mutual physical attraction and infatuation ensured that just over nine months after their wedding, their first child, Princess Victoria, was born at Buckingham Palace on 21 November 1840. Victoria's journals and letters continued to be remarkably revealing and there are some surprising admissions, particularly on her role as mother.

Baby Vicky

Following the birth of her firstborn, the Queen recorded the event in her diary: 'After a good many hours suffering, a perfect little child was born ... but alas! A girl and not a boy, as we both had so hoped and wished for.'

Shortly afterwards, Victoria wrote to her Uncle Leopold to discuss her views on pregnancy and childbirth:

I think dearest Uncle, you cannot really wish me to be the *'Mamma d'une nombreuse famille,'* for I think you will see with me the great inconvenience a large family would be to us all, and particularly to the country, independent of the hardship and inconvenience to myself; men never think, at least seldom think, what a hard task it is for us women to go through this very often.

In the same letter she also emphasized Albert's hands-on approach, while she was rather less so:

Our young lady flourishes exceedingly … I think you would be amused to see Albert dancing her in his arms; he makes a capital nurse (which I do not, and she is much too heavy for me to carry), and she already seems so happy to go to him.

Victoria saw baby Vicky, or 'Pussy' as she was known, just twice a day. The Queen had no interest in babies under the age of six months and absolutely refused to breastfeed any of her children.

The Royal Babies

Despite not wanting a large family, almost a year later, the hoped-for male heir arrived with the birth of Prince Albert Edward, or Bertie, as he was known to his family. Albert and Victoria's enthusiastic sex life meant that nine children were produced over a period of seventeen years: Vicky was born in 1840; Albert Edward in 1841; Alice in 1843; Alfred, known as Affie, in 1844; Helena, or 'Lenchen', in 1846; Louise in 1848; Arthur in 1850; Leopold in 1853, and finally, the baby of the family, Beatrice in 1857.

Queen Victoria idolized her husband and hoped to recreate him in their children. After Bertie was born on 9 November 1841, Victoria wrote to her Uncle Leopold:

> Our little boy is a wonderfully strong and large child, with very large dark blue eyes, a finely formed but somewhat large nose, and a pretty little mouth; I hope and pray he may be like his dearest Papa. He is to be called Albert, and Edward is to be his second name. Pussy, dear child, is still the great pet amongst us all, and is getting so fat and strong again. She is not at all pleased with her brother …
>
> I wonder very much who our little boy will be like. You will understand how fervent my prayers and I am sure everybody's must be, to see him resemble his angelic dearest Father in every, every respect, both in body and mind. Oh! my dearest Uncle, I am sure if you knew how happy, how blessed I feel, and how proud I feel in possessing such a perfect being as my husband … it

must gladden your heart! How happy should I be to see our child grow up just like him!

Although she was a doting and interested parent, Victoria hated being pregnant and there is a suggestion that she may have suffered from post-natal depression.

Ever honest with her Uncle Leopold, she revealed her state of mind following Bertie's birth: 'I have been suffering so from lowness that it made me quite miserable, and I know how difficult it is to fight against it.'

Victoria's firstborn, Vicky, who had been made Princess Royal in 1841, had become infinitely more appealing as she grew older, which was in stark contrast to the new baby heir to the throne:

> We found our dear little Victoria so grown and so improved, and speaking so plain, and become so independent; I think really few children are as forward as she is. She is quite a dear little companion. The Baby [Bertie] is sadly backward, but also growing, and very strong.

After the Queen and Prince Albert paid a visit to Claremont, Uncle Leopold's country house in Surrey, Victoria wrote to him on her return home:

Our Claremont trip was very enjoyable, only we missed Pussy so much; another time we shall take her with us; the dear child was so pleased to see us again, particularly dear Albert, whom she is so fond of …

… God knows how willingly I would always live with my beloved Albert and our children in the quiet and retirement of private life, and not be the constant object of observation, and of newspaper articles.

Victoria also failed to mention her son when she wrote to Leopold on the birth of her third child, Princess Alice, on 25 April 1843:

Thank God I am stronger and better this time than either time before, my nerves are so well which I am most thankful for … My adored Angel has, as usual, been all kindness and goodness, and dear Pussy a very delightful companion. She is very tender with her little sister, who is a pretty and large baby and we think will be the beauty of the family.

After the birth of their fifth child, Princess Helena, in May 1846, Victoria was unusually relaxed and conveyed a very positive perspective on life: 'Really, when one is so happy and blessed in one's home life, as I am, Politics (provided my Country is safe) must take on a second place.'

When her eighth child and youngest son, Prince Leopold, was born in 1853, Victoria was given 'that blessed chloroform' for the first time. She commented in her diary that its effects were 'soothing, quieting and delightful beyond measure'.

Osborne House

In their desire for a respectable, close-knit family, Albert and Victoria sought to distance themselves from the Queen's louche Hanoverian forebears and instead appeal to the values of the growing middle classes at home. They presented themselves as an idealized family and portraits tended to emphasize this image, starting with Edwin Landseer's informal painting of Albert, Victoria and Princess Vicky at Windsor Castle surrounded by their pet dogs in 1843.

Osborne House on the Isle of Wight was increasingly the setting for their family life. The original house was too small and so it was rebuilt for the royal couple between 1845 and 1851, based on designs by Prince Albert and the architect Thomas Cubitt. Victoria and Albert's entwined initials were everywhere – in the decorative plasterwork on the billiard room ceiling and their children's portraits, which adorned the furniture. The first photographs of Victoria, Albert and the children to be shown publicly were taken there in 1857.

In a letter to the British Prime Minister, Robert Peel, Victoria wrote about her family's happiness at spending time at Osborne House:

> We are more and more delighted with this lovely spot, the air is so pure and fresh, and … really the combination of sea, trees, woods, flowers of all kinds, the purest air … make it – to us – a perfect paradise.

Between 1853 and 1854, Prince Albert also built a Swiss-style cottage to enable the children to learn self-sufficiency. There they grew vegetables and flowers, prepared meals and were taught about the natural world.

The Children's Education

Baroness Louise Lehzen had been Victoria's childhood governess and a great support to her throughout her life. She had remained in the royal court ever since and it was the Queen's wish that the Baroness should look after her own children and take charge of the nursery. However, Albert absolutely detested Lehzen and the power she still exerted over his wife, describing the governess as 'a crazy, stupid intriguer … who regards herself as a demi-God and anyone who refuses to recognize her as such is a criminal'. His nickname for her was 'House Dragon'. Unsurprisingly, Lehzen was the catalyst for the first real row between the royal couple.

The Prince also held strong ideas about education and the way in which children should be brought up. In January 1842 both husband and wife wrote to Albert's mentor and adviser Baron Stockmar over the issue and this was one occasion when Albert triumphed, as Lehzen was dismissed and returned to Germany later that year. Albert took over the running of the nursery and devised a programme for their children's physical development, upbringing and education.

Victoria was content to let Albert manage the children's welfare while she attended to matters of state. At first, Albert found this role rewarding, and it appealed to his general interest in human behaviour as well as education. 'There is certainly a great charm, as well as deep interest, in watching the development of feelings and faculties in a little child,' he once commented.

For her part Victoria was always ready to praise their perfect father to her sons and daughters: 'None of you can ever be proud enough of being the child of such a father who has not his equal in the world, so great, so good, so faultless.'

Vicky began to learn French at eighteen months and all the children were trained in the art of conversation and how to behave at social events. Victoria and Albert often spoke German to one another and, when young, their children had German accents and all were encouraged to speak other languages. From April 1842 until December 1850, Lady Sarah Lyttelton was governess to the royal children. She had previously been lady-in-waiting to the Queen.

Despite his best efforts, the personalities of Albert's offspring sometimes got in the way of his plans for their development. Bertie – unlike his elder sister Vicky, who was exceptionally bright and eager to learn – found learning difficult. He had trouble concentrating and from an early age showed no desire to conform. His tutor Frederick Gibb found him a frustrating pupil who, when cross, would throw around books, pencils and paper. Victoria despaired of her son and his 'systematic idleness, laziness, and disregard of everything'.

When Bertie was eight years old, a phrenologist was brought in to examine the size and shape of the young boy's skull. The resulting assessment was far from reassuring, suggesting that the Prince was obstinate, stubborn and wilful.

While happy to leave their day-to-day education to Albert, Victoria tended to try to mould her children and assert her own authority over them. Each of the royal children had very distinct dispositions and over the years, not all were content to succumb to their mother's iron will. She was strict and they were afraid of her fierce temper, especially in their younger days. Victoria's volatile nature meant that she also had terrible rows with her husband, during which she would storm about, slamming doors. Albert worried about her violent rages, fearing she had inherited the madness of her grandfather King George III. He tried to encourage her to develop some self-control and more than once she wrote to him asking, 'Have I improved as I ought?'

He also repeatedly asked his wife not to be so harsh with their children and to be less critical of them. His tactful letters hint at Victoria's reaction to this advice:

> You are quite mistaken if you think I am not concerned to maintain your maternal authority with the children. On the contrary, it is my consistent care to safeguard it and preserve the warmth of the children's feeling for their Mother, and that is just the reason why I have felt it my duty to warn you of the rocks on which all our efforts are wrecked. I admit it was an error of judgment to speak to you yesterday about Alice's weeping, for I ought to have remembered the state of your nerves, but I really did not think they were shaken to the extent they have since shown themselves to be, and there was nothing in what I said to excite a healthy person to such an outburst.

Queen, Wife and Mother

Albert was always self-disciplined and supported a number of public causes and reforms. Although reluctant at first to relinquish any control, Victoria soon came to depend on her husband's wisdom, guidance and support. It was Albert who began the reform and modernization of the sovereign's role in British life, and he also played a key part in the development of the constitutional monarchy. When Robert Peel replaced Lord Melbourne as Prime Minister in 1834, Albert was given access to all the Queen's papers, helped with her correspondence and was usually present when she met with ministers. He ran the Queen's Household, office and estates, and in 1840 an act of Parliament named him regent should Victoria die before their eldest child reached the age of maturity. In 1857, Albert was formally given the title of Prince Consort, though Charles Greville, the clerk of the Privy Council, had written of him many years before, 'He is King to all intents and purposes.'

Victoria was aware that her position as Queen always placed her husband in a secondary role, that many men would find difficult. In 1858 she wrote to her eldest daughter Vicky, who that same year had married Frederick, Prince of Prussia, of her concerns in this regard:

One advantage however you all [her daughters] have over me, and that is that you are not in the anomalous position in which I am – as Queen regnant. Though dear Papa, God knows, does everything – it is a reversal of the right order of things which distresses me much and which no one, but such a perfection, such an angel as he is – could bear and carry through.

Albert was increasingly involved in social reforms including the abolition of slavery worldwide as well as educational reforms. He was the driving force behind the Great Exhibition of 1851 which opened on 1 May in the vast glass-and-iron Crystal Palace in London's Hyde Park. It proved such a success that the surplus profit of £180,000 raised was used to buy the land in South Kensington where the Natural History, Victoria & Albert and Science museums would later be built, along with educational and cultural institutions including Imperial College and the Royal Albert Hall.

Not surprisingly, with so many projects to manage, Albert's work often took him away from home, a necessity that Victoria resented: 'You cannot think how much it cost me or how completely upset I feel when Albert is away. All the numerous children are as nothing to me when he is away.'

When Vicky, who was living in Germany after marrying Frederick (known informally as Fritz) and feeling isolated in the Prussian court, wrote to her mother about how difficult she found the official meetings and constant presence of other people, Victoria was not unsympathetic, although her response was hardly tactful:

You said in your long letter that the happiest time for you – was when you were alone with Fritz; you will now understand why I often grudged you children being always there, when I longed to be alone with dearest Papa! Those are always my happiest moments!

In October 1856, when Victoria was pregnant with her last child and Vicky was already engaged to Fritz, the Queen wrote to her daughter's future mother-in-law, Princess Augusta of Prussia, about her lack of anxiety concerning the prospect of being separated from Vicky:

I see the children much less and even here, where Albert is often away all day long, I find no especial pleasure or compensation in the company of the elder children … Usually they go out with me in the afternoon (Vicky mostly, and the others also sometimes), or occasionally in the mornings when I drive or walk or ride … And only very exceptionally do I find the rather intimate intercourse with them either agreeable or easy. You will not understand this, but it is caused by various factors. Firstly, I only feel properly *à mon aise* and quite happy when Albert is with me; secondly, I am used to carrying on my many affairs quite alone; and then I have grown up all alone, accustomed to the society of adults (and never with younger) people – lastly, I still cannot get used to the fact that Vicky is almost grown up. To me she still seems the same child, who had to be kept in order and therefore must not become too intimate … And that is why the separation, although in many ways very difficult and painful for me, will not be as acute and terrible as it is in your case [the recent marriage of Augusta's own daughter and their sorrowful separation], which is really lucky.

Balmoral

Victoria and Albert first visited the Scottish Highlands in 1842 and were immediately smitten. In a letter to Lord Melbourne the Queen wrote:

The Highlands are so beautiful, and so new to me, that we are most anxious to return there again … We greatly admire the extreme beauty of Edinburgh; the situation as well as the town is most striking; and the Prince, who has seen so much, says it is the finest town he ever saw.

Two years later, writing from Windsor, Victoria told Uncle Leopold: 'I cannot reconcile myself to be here again, and pine for my dear Highlands, the hills, the pure air, the quiet, the retirement, the liberty – all – more than is right.'

The Queen's Scottish doctor, Sir James Clark, praised the healthiness of the air there and after the royal family spent a rainy, summer holiday in western Scotland in 1847, Clark commented that his son had enjoyed dry sunshine further east in Balmoral. By coincidence the lease for Balmoral Castle then became available. Albert's success in reforming the royal finances and managing the estates, as well as the improvements he had made to the farm and estate at Osborne, meant that he could afford to take on the lease, and after an unexpected bequest, he and Victoria bought the entire 17,000-acre Balmoral estate. It was to be the start of a lasting love for the place for both of them.

Victoria gave an enthusiastic description of Balmoral Castle and its location to Uncle Leopold after the family's first visit in September 1848:

> This house is small but pretty, and though the hills seen from the windows are not so fine, the scenery all around is the finest almost I have seen anywhere. It is very wild and solitary, and yet cheerful and beautifully wooded, with the river Dee running between the two sides of the hills …
>
> The climate is also dry, and in general not very cold … There is a deer forest … and on the opposite hill grouse. There is also black cock and ptarmigan.

As with Osborne, the house at Balmoral was deemed too small for the royal family and Albert set about designing a new one, with expert help provided by William Smith, City Architect of Aberdeen. Victoria laid the castle's foundation stone on 28 September 1853 and saw the new building for the first time at the end of August 1856:

> On arriving at Balmoral at seven o'clock in the evening, we found the tower finished as well as the offices, and the poor old house gone! The effect of the whole is very fine.

The Queen's journal entry for 13 October 1856 emphasized her love for Balmoral:

> Every year my heart becomes more fixed in this dear Paradise, and so much more so now, that all has become my dearest Albert's own creation, own work, own building, own laying out, as at Osborne; and his great taste, and the impress of his dear hand, have been stamped everywhere. He was very busy to-day, settling and arranging many things for next year.

Correspondence sent to Vicky and Uncle Leopold at this time reflected the same feelings and described the Queen's pleasure in walking, sketching and driving out on expeditions.

In a letter to Vicky in 1858, Victoria once again compared Windsor unfavourably to Balmoral:

How you can call Windsor 'dear' I cannot understand. It is prison-like, so large and gloomy – and for me so dull after Balmoral too, it is like jumping from day into night – fine as it is!

The Highlands and Balmoral increasingly represented an escape for the Queen and Albert. Again writing to Vicky on 9 April 1859, she revealed concerns about her ever-busy husband:

My greatest of all anxieties is that dearest Papa works too hard, wears himself quite out by all he does … If it were not for Osborne and Balmoral … I don't know what we should do.

On Pregnancy and Babies

After Vicky was married and had moved away to Prussia, Queen Victoria shared some candid views about babies in a letter to her eldest daughter:

I am no admirer of babies generally – there are exceptions – for instance (your sisters) Alice, and Beatrice were very pretty from the very first – yourself also – rather so – Arthur too … Bertie and Leopold – too frightful. Little girls are always prettier and nicer.

She also compared pregnancy to feeling like a cow:

What you say of the pride of giving life to an immortal soul is very fine, dear, but I own I cannot enter into that; I think much more of our being like a cow or a dog at such moments; when our poor nature becomes so very animal and unecstatic.

Becoming a grandmother did not make her any more enthusiastic about very young children. After a visit from her daughter-in-law, Princess Alexandra, with her new baby Princess Victoria, her fourth child with Bertie, the Queen sounded less than doting in a letter to Vicky in July 1868:

Alix continues to go on quite well, but I thought she looked pale and exhausted. The baby – a mere little red lump was all I saw; and I fear the seventh granddaughter and fourteenth grand-child becomes a very uninteresting thing – for it seems to me to go on like the rabbits in Windsor Park!

She would go on to defend her views on children when she wrote to Vicky in March 1870:

You are wrong in thinking that I am not fond of children. I am. I admire pretty ones – especially peasant children – immensely but I can't bear their being idolized and made too great objects of – or having a number of them about me, making a great noise.

On the subject of babies in general she shared the following thoughts with Vicky:

> I like them better than I did, if they are nice and pretty …
>   Abstractedly, I have no tender for them till they have become a little human; an ugly baby is a very nasty object – and the prettiest is frightful when undressed – till about four months; in short, as long as they have their big body and little limbs and that terrible frog-like action. But from four months, they become prettier and prettier.

The Queen did, however, admit to her eldest daughter that 'Your child would delight me at any age.'

A General Rule

Openly less than enthusiastic about babies she may have been, but at heart, like any parent, Victoria was not infrequently frustrated as well as impressed by her children's individuality, as revealed in this honest admission:

> You will find as your children grow up that as a rule your children are a bitter disappointment – their greatest object being to do precisely what their parents do not wish and have anxiously tried to prevent.

Her views on motherhood and the challenges of bringing up children were often frank and to the point:

> No one recognizes more than I do the blessing of having children but the anxieties and trouble, not to say sorrows, are quite as great as the blessings.
>
> Often when children have been less watched and less taken care of – the better they turn out! This is inexplicable and very annoying!

A Woman's Lot

The Queen generally seems to have thought that women got a raw deal as wives and mothers, while men remained blissfully unaware and unburdened by the strains of pregnancy and birth. She made a number of pronouncements on the theme, usually in letters to Vicky, not long after her daughter was first married:

> All marriage is such a lottery – the happiness is always an exchange – though it may be a very happy one – still the poor woman is bodily and morally the husband's slave. That always sticks in my throat. When I think of a merry, happy, and free young girl – and look at the ailing aching state a young wife is generally doomed to – which you can't deny is the penalty of marriage.

… We poor creatures are born for man's pleasure and amusement, and destined to go through endless sufferings and trials.

Men never think, at least seldom think, what a hard task it is for us women to go through this very often. God's will be done, and if He decrees that we are to have a great number of children why we must try to bring them up as useful and exemplary members of society.

Warming to her subject and hinting at her horror of breastfeeding, she wrote:

Oh! if those selfish men – who are the cause of all one's misery, only knew what their poor slaves go through! What suffering – what humiliation to the delicate feelings of a poor woman, above all a young one – especially with those nasty doctors … Especially the horrors about that peculiarly indelicate nursing (which is far worse than all the other parts).

Queen Victoria also came to the conclusion that 'being pregnant is an occupational hazard of being a wife.'

Slightly surprisingly, given her own frequent pregnancies, she made the following assertion:

I positively think ladies who are always *enceinte* quite disgusting; it is more like a rabbit or guinea-pig than anything else and really it is not very nice.

In the light of everything that women had to endure as wives and mothers, Victoria was of the steadfast opinion that 'no girl would go to the altar if she knew all.'

On the topic of marriage, the Queen had various views:

I think people really marry far too much; it is such a lottery after all, and for a poor woman a very doubtful happiness.

I think unmarried people are very often very happy – certainly more so than married people who don't live happily together of which there are so many instances.

But despite these pronouncements, she did admit that 'Being married gives one one's position like nothing else can.'

With regard to her own marriage, she was unequivocally positive. On the eve of her wedding anniversary in February 1858, Queen Victoria shared her thoughts in a letter to her Uncle Leopold:

Tomorrow is the eighteenth anniversary of my blessed marriage, which has brought such universal blessings on this country and Europe! For what has not my beloved and perfect Albert done? Raised monarchy to the highest pinnacle of respect, and rendered it popular beyond what it ever was in this country!

Sons and Daughters

Sons and Daughters

Alongside creating the ideal family, Albert and Victoria had high hopes for a harmonious Europe with an Anglo-German dynasty centred on their family. It was Victoria's wish that her children should marry for love as she herself had done, but that did not mean the match could not also be politically advantageous. It was generally assumed that suitable candidates would be found among the royal houses of Europe. A British subject, even an aristocrat, was simply not royal and failed to offer the same opportunities for foreign alliance.

Loyal and upright, Albert was devoted to his wife and they both considered sexual morality to be vitally important. This was a cherished value that was to cause more than a little conflict with both Bertie and Affie as they entered adulthood.

To advance their vision of a pro-English Germany, a meeting was arranged at Balmoral in 1855 between Princess Victoria, the Princess Royal, and Frederick

(Fritz), Prince of Prussia, who was heir to the German throne. The couple swiftly fell in love. The marriage eventually took place in January 1858 at the Chapel Royal of St James's Palace in London and they moved to Berlin immediately afterwards. Vicky was just seventeen and both Victoria and Albert were devastated to lose their beloved, clever, eldest daughter. Vicky privately confessed to her mother, 'I think it will kill me to take leave of Papa!'

In a change of heart from her letter to Princess Augusta of Prussia in October 1856, when Vicky and Fritz were engaged and Victoria was sanguine about the prospect of being separated from her eldest daughter, the Queen admitted to Uncle Leopold:

> I feel it is terrible to give up one's poor child, and feel very nervous for the coming time, and for the departure. After all it is like taking a lamb to be sacrificed.

There was the sudden realization that Vicky would be living abroad: 'She will return but for a short time, almost as a visitor.'

Victoria also considered that her daughter might be much changed on her future return to England: 'She will no longer be an innocent girl – but a wife – and – perhaps, this time next year already a mother!'

Letters to Vicky

Vicky's move to the Prussian court marked the start of a regular correspondence between the Princess and her parents. She wrote weekly to her father detailing court life and politics. The Queen, meanwhile, wrote almost daily letters to her eldest daughter, whom she still tried to direct and control from afar.

Altogether more than 8,000 letters were exchanged between mother and daughter. Queen Victoria's in particular are remarkably candid and unguarded, perhaps because she sometimes felt as if she were communicating with 'my sister rather than my child'. Unlike her journals, her letters escaped Beatrice's later editing and transcribing, and so offer a unique insight into the Queen's thoughts and character.

Victoria wrote the first of her letters on 2 February 1858, the day that Vicky departed for Germany:

> An hour is already past since you left – and I trust that you are recovering a little, but then will come that awful separation from dearest Papa! How I wish that was over for you, my beloved child! … Yes it is cruel, very cruel – very trying for parents to give up their beloved children, and to see them go away from the happy peaceful

home – where you used all to be around us! … Poor dear Alice, whose sobs must have gone to your heart – is sitting near me writing to you … Dearest, dearest child, may every blessing attend you both.

Two days later, the Queen's letter to Vicky revealed how she was coping with her daughter's absence:

I am better today, but my first thoughts on waking were very sad – and the tears are ever coming to my eyes and ready to flow again … Everything recalls you to our mind, and in every room we shall have your picture.

On 5 February, Victoria's heartache showed no sign of abating:

You wrote dearest Papa such a beautiful letter, it made me cry so much, as indeed everything does. I don't find I get any better … God bless you for your dear warm affectionate heart and for your love to your adored father. That will bring blessings on you both! How he deserves your worship – your confidence. What a pride to be his child as it is for me to be his wife!

Victoria's letters continued with advice, even down to the type of writing paper that Vicky should use. She also issued the odd reprimand when her daughter failed to answer her questions in what she considered to be the right way. While the Queen obviously wanted Vicky to be happy, there is a hint of petulance at any suggestion she might be *too* happy in her new home:

Pray do answer my questions, my dearest child, else you will be as bad as Bertie used to be, and it keeps me in such a fidget. I asked you several questions on a separate paper about health, cold sponging – temperature of your rooms etc. and you have not answered one! You should just simply and shortly answer them one by one and then there could be no mistake about them. My good dear child is a little unmethodical and unpunctual still … Are you happier than at Windsor? I thought that you could not be. Bertie is shocked at your liking everything so much.

That you are so happy is a great happiness and great comfort to us and yet it gives me a pang, as I said once before to see and feel my own child so much happier than she ever was before, with another … You know, my dearest, that I never admit any other wife can be as happy as I am – so I can admit no comparison for I maintain Papa is unlike anyone who lives or ever lived and will live.

Though she may have been entrusted with many of her mother's confidences, even Vicky did not escape her personal reproaches:

Do you know that you've got into a habit of writing so many words with a capital letter at the beginning? With nouns that would not signify so much, but you do it with verbs and adjectives, which is very incorrect, dear, and would shock other people if you wrote to them so.

I wish you for the future to adopt the plan of beginning your letters with the following sort of headings. Yesterday, or the day before, we did so and so, went here or there, and then where you spent the evening.

At times, the Queen adopted an even more pointed approach:

Your answers yesterday by telegram are not quite satisfactory and you don't say whether your cold is better, or not. Were you feverishly unwell with it, or not? I get terribly fidgeted at not knowing what is really the matter … I really hope you are not getting fat again. Avoid eating soft, pappy things or drinking much. You know how that fattens.

Prince Albert obviously thought that Victoria wrote too often to her daughter, which in turn forced Vicky to send regular replies:

If you knew how Papa scolds me for (as he says) making you write! And he goes further, he says that I write far too often to you, and that it would be much better if I wrote only once a week! ... I think however Papa is wrong and you do like to hear from home often. When you do write to Papa again just tell him what you feel and wish ... for I assure you Papa has snubbed me several times very sharply on the subject and when one writes in spite of fatigues and trouble to be told it bores the person to whom you write, it is rather too much!

When the Queen learned that Vicky had twisted her ankle at the beginning of May 1858, she reacted as if her daughter had carelessly injured herself just to upset her mother:

How dreadfully vexed, worried and fidgety I am at this untoward sprain I can't tell you! How could you do it? I am sure you had too high heeled boots! I am haunted with your lying in a stuffy room in that dreadful old Schloss – without fresh air and alas! naturally without exercise and am beside myself.

At other times, the Queen made light of any problems Vicky might have and was wholly unsympathetic. When the sprain failed to improve, Victoria was less than supportive: 'I fear you exaggerate as you so often used to do. Others who do not know your disposition think you are really ill! Which you are not!'

However, this was nothing compared to her response to the news that Vicky was pregnant on 26 May 1858: 'The horrid news … has upset us dreadfully. The more so as I feel certain almost it will come to nothing.' Not quite the expected reaction from a proud prospective grandmother.

Victoria had previously advised her daughter to avoid pregnancy too early in her married life, effectively saying that Vicky's birth had ruined the first years of her own marriage:

> I cannot tell you how happy I am that you are not in an unenviable position. I never can rejoice by hearing that a poor young thing is pulled down by this trial. Though I quite admit the comfort and blessing good and amiable children are – though they are also an awful plague and anxiety for which they show one so little gratitude very often! What made me so miserable was – to have the first two years of my married life utterly spoilt by this occupation! I could enjoy nothing – not travel or go about with dear Papa and if I had waited a year, as I hope you will, it would have been different.

After coming to terms with her daughter's imminent motherhood, however, the Queen slightly softened her attitude:

> I delight in the idea of being a grandmamma; to be that at 39 (D.V.) [God willing] and to look and feel young is great fun … I think of my next birthday being spent with my children and a grandchild. It will be a treat!

With the birth of her first baby fast approaching Vicky was warned by her mother not to talk to other women about what to expect, 'particularly abroad, where so much more fuss is made of a very natural and usual thing'. There was not much consolation for the Princess afterwards either. Her labour dragged on for thirty-six hours, with no pain relief, and a fumbled forceps delivery permanently injured baby Wilhelm's arm. Her firstborn would grow up to become Kaiser Wilhelm II, who would be responsible for setting Germany on a course of action that ultimately led to the First World War.

The Queen's reassuring but dismissive response to her daughter's unpleasant experience was, 'But don't be alarmed for the future. It can never be so bad again.'

Once the child was born, Victoria was at pains to counsel Vicky against lavishing too much attention on him:

> I know you will not forget, dear, your promise not to indulge in 'baby worship', or to neglect your other duties in becoming a nurse … as my dear child is a little disorderly in regulating her time, I fear you might lose a great deal of it, if you overdid the passion for the

nursery. No lady, and still less a Princess, is fit for her husband or her position, if she does that.

Looking back on her own feelings compared to those of her daughter, she revealed, 'I never cared for you near as much as you seem to about the baby; I care much more for the younger ones (poor Leopold perhaps excepted).'

In another letter Victoria asked Vicky not to tell her younger sister Alice too much about pregnancy or childbirth, again clearly imposing her own opinion upon her:

> Let me caution, dear child, again, to say as little as you can on these subjects before Alice (who has already heard much more than you ever did) for she has the greatest horror of having children, and would rather have none – just as I was when a girl and when I first married – so I am very anxious she should know as little about the inevitable miseries as possible; so don't forget, dear.

The Queen also expressed her intentions about the futures of her other daughters:

> I really think I shall never let your sisters marry – certainly not to be so constantly away and see so little of their parents – as till now you have done … It really makes me shudder when I look around at all your sweet, happy,

unconscious sisters – and think that I must give them up too – one by one!!

Women of Letters

Throughout all the letters, mother and daughter discuss their taste in books and recommend titles to one another. Victoria tells Vicky she is reading Charlotte Brontë's *Jane Eyre* aloud to Albert and explains that although Elizabeth Barrett Browning's poem *Aurora Leigh* may seem 'dreadfully coarse', she thinks it 'an incredible book for a lady to have written'. Vicky was unimpressed. Just three days later she wrote back to say that she considered it 'thoroughly without taste and poetry'.

A fan of novelist George Eliot, the Queen admitted she had been moved by *The Mill on the Floss*: 'I must say it made a deep impression on me. The writing and the descriptions of feelings is wonderful and painful!'

Anthony Trollope, however, was not so favoured by Victoria:

I have not read 'Barchester Towers' all through, but I am told it is not meant to be so ill-natured. But I don't like reading it aloud to Papa as there was not enough romance in it. The people I could not interest myself in.

In April 1859, the two swapped views on the works of William Shakespeare. The Queen wrote:

By the by you went to see the 'Merry Wives'; you must have found it very coarse; even I have never had courage to go to see it – having always been told how very coarse it was – for your adored Shakespeare is dreadful in that respect and many things have to be left out in many of his plays.

A few days later Victoria returned to the subject of theatre, and the French:

With regard to what you say about Shakespeare, I quite agree. You need not be afraid of seeing Faust; I am as bad and shy as anyone, matron as I am, about these things – and it is so beautiful that really one does not feel put out by it. I advise you to see it, dear. Also as regards the French plays – you should go; there are many – indeed quantities of charming little plays – and dear Papa – who you know is anything but favourable to the French – used to delight in going to the French play – more than to any other, and we used for many years … to go continually and enjoyed it excessively. It is such good practice for the language. So, I hope, dear, you will go. One's dislike to a nation need not prevent one's admiring and being amused by what is good, clever and amusing in it.

Despite the Queen's best efforts to shape her daughter in her own image, Vicky was very much her father's daughter in terms of intellect. Clever, and an independent thinker, she shared Albert's belief in an enlightened Europe centred on Germany. Her mother viewed her liberal-conservatism with some scepticism and showed concern that her daughter was developing increasingly radical ideas, as noted in a letter of 1883:

> Now let me soothe your feelings of injustice about my 'little hit' at your being a Radical. I will yield to none in true liberalism, but republicanism and destructiveness are no true liberalism … If you lived here and saw and understood all that goes on you would see that these so-called, but not really 'liberal' ideas are very mischievous.

Son and Heir

Victoria despaired of her eldest son Bertie. Her letters to Vicky constantly refer to his many failings:

> [Bertie was] the only one of all the children, who neither drew, wrote, played or did anything whatever to show his affection …
>
> He vexes us much. There is not a particle of reflection, or even attention to anything but dress! Not the slightest desire to learn …

Aside from his perceived failings, Victoria was even disparaging about her son's personality: 'I own I find him very dull; his three other brothers are all so amusing and communicative.'

Sometimes, the Queen could not even bring herself to write about him: 'Oh! Bertie alas! That is too sad a subject to enter on.'

In spring 1859, the Queen noted a modicum of progress in her son, though her phrasing was less than positive: 'But oh! it is the improvement of such a poor or still more idle intellect.'

She seems to have genuinely feared that he would never be fit for his future position as King: 'His only safety and the country's – is in his implicit reliance in every thing, on dearest Papa, that perfection of human beings!'

In another letter to her daughter from April 1860, Victoria wondered why Vicky did not answer her criticisms of Bertie, and those of her other brothers:

You don't once enter into any of my observations upon Bertie? It is such a proof of my confidence in you when I speak to you so openly about your brothers – that your silence seems strange to me. Poor Bertie, I pity him; but I blame him too, for that idleness is really sinful.

The Queen was also highly critical of her eldest son's appearance:

He is not at all in good looks; his nose and mouth are too enormous and he pastes his hair down to his head, and wears his clothes frightfully – he really is anything but good-looking.

Handsome I cannot think him with that painfully small and narrow head, those immense features and total want of chin.

Even his voice made his mother 'so nervous I could hardly bear it'.

After a visit to her family in England in early summer, 1859, Vicky felt moved to defend her brother in a letter to her mother:

Only one thing pains me … and that is the relation between you and Bertie! In the railway carriage going to Dover, I thought so much about it, and wished I could have told you how kindly, nicely and properly and even sensibly he spoke, his heart is very capable of affection, of warmth and feeling …

Despite conveying such heartfelt support for her brother, her arguments failed to persuade the Queen, who continued much as before.

Writing to Vicky about the need to find a princess to marry Bertie, in an earlier letter of March 1858, Victoria had suggested that ideally the potential bride should be a couple of years younger than him and 'pretty, quiet and clever and sensible'. Princess Alexandra of Denmark finally emerged as a leading candidate.

In February 1861, Victoria wrote to Vicky on a quest for information:

> As regards Princess Alexandra of D, you could surely … find out everything about her education and general character … The looks and manner we know are excellent, and whether she seems very *outré* Danish.
>
> The subject is so important – the choice so circumscribed, that I am sure you will kindly set about at once finding out all these things. It is so very important – with the peculiar character we have to deal with. The Princess of Meiningen, he did not like, and she is not strong; Marie of the Netherlands is clever and ladylike, but too plain and not strong, and poor Addy [Princess Alexandrine, niece of the King of Prussia] not clever or pretty.

By summer 1861, Albert was arranging a suitable dynastic marriage between Bertie and Princess Alexandra of Denmark. In line with their image as the ideal family, Victoria and Albert were keen to portray this as a love match and it was important to both of them that Bertie should appear chaste.

Unbeknown to his parents, while at university in

Cambridge, Bertie had met the hard-drinking, partying and gambling set, including Charles, Lord Carrington, who was to become his friend for life. After one late-night party in 1861, Carrington had introduced the young Prince to a part-time actress called Nellie Clifden. She had then visited his rooms in Cambridge overnight. That summer, while away training with the Grenadier Guards at Curragh Camp in County Kildare, fellow officers had arranged for her to travel to Ireland to see Bertie again. Notes in his appointment book mention trysts with 'NC' on 6, 9 and 10 September 1861.

News of the affair reached the Prince's horrified parents two months later. Albert wrote his son a damning letter, while Victoria was at first inclined to blame others, writing, 'Wicked wretches have led our poor innocent boy into a scrape.'

She was to be far less understanding after Albert travelled to meet with Bertie in Cambridge in late November, talking and walking with him for hours in the rain. This was believed to have caused the chill and the start of the fever which worsened over the following days, eventually leading to Albert's death in mid-December. The grief-stricken Queen never really forgave her son for what she referred to as his 'fall', maintaining that Albert had been 'killed by that dreadful business'. Bertie's relationship with Nellie Clifden was soon over, though it was to be only the first of many affairs throughout his life.

Two weeks after Albert died, Victoria's comments to Vicky are revealing:

Thank dear Fritz ... for all he did and said to poor, unhappy Bertie. Tell him that Bertie (oh! that boy – much as I pity I never can or shall look at him without a shudder as you may imagine) does not know, that I know all, (beloved Papa told him that I could not be told 'the disgusting details') that I try to employ and use him – but I am not hopeful ... This dreadful cross kills me.

In July 1862, Victoria wrote to Vicky with an update on her brother's situation:

Poor Bertie! – he is very affectionate and dutiful but he is very trying. The idleness is the same – and there is a great roughness of manner to his brothers and sisters which must be got the better of. Still he is most anxious to do what is right, that is every thing. But his idleness and 'desoeuvrement' [aimlessness], his listlessness and want of attention are great, and cause me much anxiety.

In truth, whether Victoria recognized it or not, her eldest son had inherited not her beloved Albert's personality but in some respects her own. Like her Hanoverian forebears, she loved sex, had a terrible temper and a big appetite for food and life. More positively, both mother and son were at least blessed with a good measure of common sense.

A Noble Resolve

The death of Albert was to have a huge impact on the children's relationship with their mother. She had always been the sterner more distant parent. Her mood swings and temper were unpredictable, and the children lived in fear of provoking her anger or displeasure. Albert had disciplined his children and on occasion caned his sons, as corporal punishment was not unusual at the time, but he always enjoyed their company, treated them as equals and they were in no doubt that he loved them.

After her husband's death, Victoria's darker side intensified. She relied on the younger girls' constant presence and sought to control all her children to an even greater degree. She was also absolutely determined to carry out Albert's objectives in every detail, particularly with regard to their children, and woe betide anyone who tried to stand in her way.

On 24 December 1861 she wrote to her Uncle Leopold, making her intentions very clear:

> I am also anxious to repeat one thing, and that one is my firm resolve, my irrevocable decision, viz. that his wishes – his plans – about everything, his views about every thing are to be my law! And no human power will make me swerve from what he decided and wished – and I look to you to support and help me in this. I

apply this particularly as regards our children – Bertie, etc. – for whose future he had traced everything so carefully. I am also determined that no one person, may he be ever so good, ever so devoted among my servants – is to lead or guide or dictate to me. I know how he would disapprove it. And I live on with him, for him; in fact I am only outwardly separated from him, and only for a time …

Though miserably weak and utterly shattered, my spirit rises when I think any wish or plan of his is to be touched or changed, or I am to be made to do anything. I know you will help me in my utter darkness. It is but for a short time, and then I go – never, never to part! Oh! that blessed, blessed thought! He seems so near to me, so quite my own now, my precious darling!

The Prince and Princess of Wales

In line with the wishes of his father and mother, Bertie proposed to Princess Alexandra of Denmark in September 1862 at the Royal Castle of Laeken in Belgium, the home of Victoria's uncle, King Leopold I. The Queen was most impressed by her future daughter-in-law's appearance as her journal entry reveals:

[Princess Alexandra] looked lovely, in a black dress, nothing in her hair, and curls on either side, which hung over her shoulders, her hair turned back off her beautiful forehead. Her whole appearance was one of the greatest charm, combined with simplicity and perfect dignity. I gave her a little piece of white heather, which Bertie gave me at Balmoral, and I told her I hoped it would bring her luck. Dear Uncle Leopold, who sat near me, was charmed with her. Very tired, and felt low and agitated.

A few days after the proposal, Victoria wrote to her eldest daughter of her own bittersweet feelings, which were not altogether the sentiments one would expect a mother to share:

> [Alexandra] is a dear, lovely being – whose bright image seems to float – mingled with darling Papa's – before my poor eyes – dimmed with tears! Dearest child! this very prospect of opening happiness of married life for our poor Bertie – while I thank God for it – yet wrings my poor heart, which seems transfixed with agonies of longing! I am alas! Not old – and my feelings are strong and warm; my love is ardent.

The couple were married on 10 March 1863 at St George's Chapel, Windsor Castle. Bertie was twenty-one years old and Alexandra was eighteen. Photographs of the day show the Queen apparently ignoring everyone and staring stonily at a bust of Albert.

Bertie and Alexandra lived not far from Buckingham Palace at Marlborough House in St James's, and at first Victoria expected to exert the same influence over her son that she had before his marriage. She attempted to set a timetable for their lives and placed spies in the young couple's household. But Bertie was resourceful and managed to evade his mother's control. The glamorous pair established a lively social life and enjoyed entertaining on a lavish scale in their London home, and at Sandringham House in Norfolk, their country estate.

After Bertie's marriage, relations with his mother seemed to improve slightly, although the Queen could still be bitingly critical. Victoria alternated between lavish praise and criticism of Alexandra, whom she usually called Alix: 'She is one of those sweet creatures who seem to come from the skies to help and bless poor mortals and brighten for a time their path!'

While generally approving of her 'nice – so sympathetic – quiet, but gay and clever' daughter-in-law, the Queen disliked the fact that she enjoyed hunting and also frowned upon the young couple's constant socializing.

To Vicky, the usual recipient of her mother's private opinions, she wrote the following in spring 1863:

Poor Alix is not I fear reasonable or careful of her health and I must speak seriously to both else there will be mishaps and an end to good health and possibly to much of their happiness. It is amusing to see how Bertie keeps her in order (not in an improper way) and takes care of her ... She will require care, that I am sure of.

... I am quite astonished at Bertie's improvement. Dear Alix felt the parting from her parents very much, but she is always calm and sweet and gentle and lovely. Very clever I don't think she is, but she is right-minded and sensible and straightforward. Dagmar [Alexandra's sister] is cleverer, and would I am sure be very fit for the position in Russia [the wife of Tsar Alexander of Russia]; she is a very nice girl.

Bertie and Alix are here since Saturday. I do so wonder how she can be happy. He has let himself down to his bad manners again. She is dear and good but I think looks far from strong and will never be able to bear the London season unless she has but few late nights. She is but 18 and has gone through so much.

A few weeks later, the Queen was even more barbed:

I fear there is none [no sign of pregnancy] with Alix and though to be sure, unintellectual children which one might fear with B.'s children, would be a great misfortune, it would be very sad if they had none, and I sometimes fear they won't. Are you aware that Alix has the smallest head ever seen? I dread that – with his small empty brain – very much for future children. The doctor says that Alix's head goes in, in the most extraordinary way just beyond the forehead: I wonder what phrenologists would say.

In May 1863, the Queen wrote to Vicky detailing concerns about her daughter-in-law's health, particularly regarding her increasing deafness which was caused by a hereditary condition:

> Poor dear [Alexandra], she looks so sallow and is losing her '*fraicheur*'. Alas! she is deaf and everyone observes it, which is a sad misfortune. Strong she is not, and they overtire her too much.

By June 1863, Victoria was comparing her eldest son unfavourably to his father:

> Bertie and Alix left Frogmore today – both looking as ill as possible. We are all seriously alarmed about her – for though Bertie writes and says he is so anxious to take care of her, he goes on going out every night till she will become a skeleton, and hopes there cannot be!! I am quite unhappy about it. Oh! how different poor, foolish Bertie is to adored Papa whose gentle, loving, wise, motherly care of me when he was not [yet] 21 exceeded everything.

She also confided in Vicky her complete lack of confidence and distrust of Bertie's abilities as future monarch. She despised his playboy image and apparent lack of intellect:

I fear she [Alexandra] will never be what she would be had she a clever, sensible and well-informed husband, instead of a very weak and terribly frivolous one! Oh! what will become of the poor country when I die! I foresee, if B. succeeds, nothing but misery – for he never reflects or listens for a moment and he [would] do anything he was asked and spend his life in one whirl of amusements as he does now! It makes me very sad and angry.

In fact, Bertie, as Edward VII, went on to be a very successful King. He was charming, sociable and wisely tactful when it came to diplomacy, and remained popular with the public. He carried on the work that his father had begun in modernizing the British monarchy to make it relevant and appealing in a modern age, when across Europe the positions of other royal houses were far from popular or secure.

Despite the Queen's misgivings, Alexandra and Bertie had six children. Their first, Albert Victor, was born in January 1864, and the Princess of Wales was a devoted mother. Their head nurse commented: 'She was in her glory when she could run up to the nursery, put on a flannel apron, wash the children herself and see them asleep in their little beds.'

What's in a Name?

After the birth of Albert Victor, Victoria went to stay with Alexandra at Frogmore House at Windsor, her insistence on helping not entirely welcome. She wrote to Bertie just after the birth to make clear her views:

> I wish now to say a few words again about the names, sponsors, and christening … I quite agree to its being best for the people of London that they should not be deprived of the honour and gratification of having some event in town; and by having it … in the private chapel at Buckingham Palace, I think I shall be able to be present, and hold the dear baby myself … As regards the names, if others besides Albert Victor are added … you must take dear Uncle Leopold's also. You could not give King Christian's and the Landgrave's without also giving Uncle Leopold's. I would advise reserving Edward for a second or third son. [The baby was actually christened Albert Victor Christian Edward].
>
> Respecting your own names, and the conversation we had, I wish to repeat, that it was beloved Papa's wish, as well as mine, that you should be called by both, when you become King, and it would be impossible for you to drop your Father's. It would be monstrous, and Albert alone, as you truly and amiably say, would not do, as there can be only one Albert! You

will begin a new line ... for it will be the Saxe-Coburg line united with the Brunswick ... and your son will be known by the two others, as you are by Albert Edward!

At the time of Albert Victor's arrival, Victoria was particularly concerned about family names and loyalties as there was a crisis in Europe over Germany's claim to the Duchies of Schleswig and Holstein which were then ruled by Denmark. She expressed her thoughts in a letter to Vicky:

Oh! if Bertie's wife was only a good German and not a Dane! Not, as regards the influence of the politics but as regards the peace and harmony in the family! It is terrible to have the poor boy on the wrong side, and aggravates my suffering greatly.

The Queen was just as opinionated after the birth of their second child, the future King George V, who was christened George Frederick Ernest Albert. She wrote to her son on 13 June 1865:

I fear I cannot admire the names you propose to give the Baby. I had hoped for some fine old name. Frederic is, however, the best of the two, and I hope you will call him so; George only came over with the Hanoverian family. However, if the dear child grows up good and wise, I shall not mind what his name is. Of course you will add Albert at the end, like your brothers, as you know we settled long ago that all dearest Papa's male

English descendants should bear that name, to mark our line, just as I wish all the girls to have Victoria at the end of theirs! I lay great stress on this.

Much to her frustration, Bertie and Alexandra tended to carry on as they had planned regardless of the Queen's wishes. Each of Alexandra's babies was apparently born prematurely and there is some suggestion that the Princess deliberately misled the Queen, giving later due dates to ensure that her majesty was not present at their births.

Two years later, the Queen shared her current thoughts on Alexandra with Vicky: 'Dear Alix I don't think improved. She is grown a little grand, I think, and we never get more intimate or nearer to each other.'

On another occasion she went so far as to express sympathy for her eldest son:

> I am sorry for Bertie; I don't think she makes his home comfortable; she is never ready for breakfast – not being out of her room till 11 often, and poor Bertie breakfasts alone and then she alone. I think it gets much worse instead of better; it makes me unhappy and anxious.

In 1867, Alexandra became dangerously ill with rheumatic fever during the birth of her third child, Princess Louise. She recovered but was left with a permanent limp and for some months could walk only with the aid of two walking sticks. The Queen, as usual, wrote to Vicky about her daughter-in-law's progress:

> Really Bertie is so full of good and amiable qualities that it makes one forget and overlook much that one would wish different. Dearest Alix walks about, and up and down stairs – everywhere with the help of one or two sticks – but of course very slowly. She even gets in and out of a carriage, but it is a sad sight to see her thus and to those who did not see her so ill as we did, when one really did not dare to hope she would get better, it is sad and touching to see. She is very thin and looks very frail but very pretty, and is so good and patient under this heavy trial. The poor leg is completely stiff and it remains to be seen whether it will ever get quite right again.

Princess Alexandra's style was very much admired and copied by the British public and as a result some women even went so far as to imitate the 'Alexandra limp'.

Alice

In December 1860, Queen Victoria wrote to her Uncle Leopold with her usual swiftness about the proposed marriage of her third child Alice to Prince Louis of Hesse-Darmstadt. Princess Vicky had suggested Louis, along with his brother Henry, as possible suitors for her sister. The Queen had been impressed by both young men, but it was obvious that Alice and Louis got on especially well together:

> My beloved Uncle – I have to thank you for two most kind letters of the 4th and 7th. Your kind interest in our dear child's happiness – your approval of this marriage of our dear Alice, which, I cannot deny, has been for long an ardent wish of mine, and just therefore I feared so much it never would come to pass, gives us the greatest pleasure. Now – that all has been so happily settled, and that I find the young man so very charming – my joy, and my deep gratitude to God are very great! He is so loveable, so very young, and like one of our own children – not the least in the way – but a dear pleasant, bright companion, full of fun and spirits, and I am sure will be a great comfort to us, besides being an excellent husband to our dear, good Alice, who, though radiant with joy and much in love (which well she may be), is as quiet and sensible as possible.

The engagement became official in April 1861, but Alice's wedding was not to take place until 1 July 1862. She nursed her father during his final illness in December 1861 and then effectively became her mother's unofficial secretary for six months while the grieving Queen was incapable of attending to her own affairs. Alice was her mother's emotional support and took charge of Victoria's official business, acting as intermediary between the government and the Queen.

At Victoria's insistence, the wedding went ahead just as Albert had planned, in a private ceremony in the dining room of Osborne House. The weather was grey and windy and the Queen wrote in her journal of her sadness:

> Scarcely got any sleep … I in my 'sad cap' [her widow's cap] as Baby [Beatrice] calls it, most sad on such a day, went down with our four boys, Bertie and Affie leading me. It was a terrible moment for me … I sat all the time in an armchair, Bertie and Affie close to me … I restrained my tears, and had a great struggle all through, but remained calm.

The next day she wrote to Vicky in Prussia:

> Poor Alice's wedding (more like a funeral than a wedding) is over and she is a wife! I say God bless her – though a dagger is plunged in my bleeding, desolate heart when I hear from her this morning that she is 'proud and happy' to be Louis' wife! I feel what I had, what I hoped to have for at least 20 years more and what I can only have in another world again. All that has passed since December 14 seems gone – forgotten. What I shall not forget is Alice herself, and her wonderful bearing – such calmness, self-possession and dignity, and how really beautiful she

looked … I sat the whole time in an armchair, with our four boys near me; Bertie and Affie led me down stairs. The latter sobbed all through and afterwards – dreadfully.

Despite the unfailing support that Alice had given her mother following her father's death, Queen Victoria was to change her opinion of her 'most dear, good child'. Far from Alice being her trusted confidante – 'there is not a thing I cannot tell her, she knows everything and is the best element one can have in the family!' – relations between mother and daughter deteriorated to such an extent that at one point Victoria called Alice 'the real devil in the family'.

In Victoria's eyes, Alice's character was transformed after her marriage, and not for the better. In January 1867 The Queen wrote to Vicky about recent events concerning her younger daughter:

I wish to say a few more words in confidence about Alice … I told you in my last letter that she had, from the time when she married and came back here, not been liked in the house from her ordering and commanding and from her want of tact and discretion … Well, when Alice came the last two times she grumbled about everything – and Louis also sometimes – the rooms, the hours, wanting to make me do this and that and preventing my being read to of a evening as Louis would come and he always fell asleep.

In July that year, the Queen revealed that 'Alice is very amiable but she and Louis are no comfort. They are not quiet. Alice is very fond of amusing herself and of fine society and I think they do everyone harm. They ruined Affie.' This directly contradicted the sentiments she had expressed to Vicky almost four years earlier in November 1863:

> Dear Alice and Louis are a great comfort to me – so good and kind and so quiet; he is so improved, really so excellent, with much decision and firmness of character. I do love him dearly. Oh! if the boys (our sons) had his golden heart – especially Affie – who is a slippery youth, for I never feel sure (alas!) of what he says.

The Princes and Princesses tended to rise or fall in their mother's affections according to how closely they had followed her wishes. As one became her favourite another was usually relegated to a lesser position. The real issue the Queen had with Alice was that she had independent ideas and disobeyed her mother. She was interested in the position of women and the changes that were happening in society. She was also drawn to medicine and nursing in direct defiance of Victoria, treating wounded soldiers and founding the Princess Alice Women's Guild in Hesse, which effectively took over the running of the military hospitals during the Austro-Prussian war of 1866, and so whenever Alice asked her mother for money or medical supplies for her nursing guild, she was ignored. But it was Alice's interest in gynaecology that caused her mother most concern and led to Victoria's strict warning to Princess Louise after her marriage in 1871: 'Don't let Alice pump you. Be very silent and cautious about your "interior".'

The Queen was also appalled and disgusted by Alice's, as well as Vicky's, insistence on breastfeeding their babies, which was becoming the norm even among middle- and upper-class mothers. Victoria commanded her daughters not to breastfeed and when she realized they had disobeyed her, she wrote, 'It does make my hair stand on end to think that my two daughters should turn into cows.' She took her revenge by naming one of the royal dairy cows 'Princess Alice'.

In December 1878, Alice contracted diphtheria in Hesse. She had spent the past month nursing her family through the disease before falling ill herself. She died on 14 December, the seventeenth anniversary of her father's death. Victoria was swift to praise her daughter's character, all past disagreements forgotten:

It was too awful! I had so hoped against hope. Went to Bertie's sitting-room. His despair was great. As I kissed him, he said, 'It is the good who are always taken.' That this dear, talented, distinguished, tender-hearted, noble-minded, sweet child, who behaved so admirably during her father's illness and afterwards, in supporting me, and helping me in every possible way, should be called back to her father on this very anniversary, seems almost incredible and mysterious!

Affie

Alfred, or Affie as he was known in the family, was born in 1844. Intelligent and mechanically minded from a young age, he was a promising child and a favourite with his father. When he was eleven and Bertie was fourteen, the two boys were caught smoking together. The decision was then made to separate the brothers – to avoid Affie following Bertie's bad example. Affie lived away in Edinburgh for a time with his tutor and while there taught himself to play the violin. It was his wish to join the Royal Navy and after passing his exams he became a midshipman on HMS *Euryalus* at the age of fourteen in summer 1858.

Earlier that year, Victoria was full of praise for her second son: 'Affie is going on admirably ... and oh! when I see him and Arthur and look at ... ! (You know what I mean!) [i.e. the disappointing Bertie].'

After Affie had left them to embark upon his naval voyage, she wrote:

Dearest Affie is gone; and it will be 10 months probably before we shall see his dear face which shed sunshine over the whole house, from his amiable, happy, merry temper; again he was much upset at leaving and sobbed bitterly, and I fear the separation from dear Papa will have been equally trying.

But she was soon quick to criticize Affie's handwriting, which fell short of the required standard:

> His letters of which he has given us only three specimens are too shockingly and disgracefully written. Strange that both the boys should write so ill – and that all the girls so well.

In early 1860, Affie was home on leave to the joy of both parents, and again Victoria felt that the difference between him and Bertie was marked:

> Dear Affie is our great delight so full of fun and conversation and so full of anxiety to learn … such steam power, such energy it is such a great pleasure to see this – but the contrast with someone else is sad.
>
> Affie is, I really think beautiful (excepting Papa who is much more so) – but it is such a darling, handsome, round face.

At the age of seventeen, Affie returned home briefly on his father's death, but he was soon back at sea. From then on his relationship with his mother deteriorated abruptly, beyond repair. When news that Affie had slept with a young woman in Malta reached the Queen, she was appalled. In October 1862, Victoria wrote to Vicky to share her despair:

> Affie has dealt a heavy blow to my weak and shattered frame and I feel quite bowed down with it. In Affie's case – there is not a particle of excuse, his conduct was both heartless and dishonourable. But he does feel it though he can't, poor boy, give utterance ever to any thing. But his great palour [sic], thinness, his subdued tone, and his excessive anxiety by every little act to give me pleasure, to do what I like and wish, show me he feels enough. I had wished not to see him … but for the world it was necessary … It was very trying.

The only thing that caused Victoria to relent a little was Affie's resemblance to dearest Albert, though it was a pity that his morals did not match his father's: 'But he is indeed in many things wonderfully like adored Papa – and his figure is a miniature of that angel! Oh! that he were as pure!'

By autumn 1866 the Queen was generally more affectionate towards her oldest son, while relations with Affie continued to deteriorate:

> Affie makes me very unhappy; he hardly ever comes near me, is reserved, touchy, vague and wilful and I distrust him completely. All the good derived from his stay in Germany has disappeared. He is quite a stranger to me. Bertie, on the other hand, is really very amiable.

In March 1868, while on a visit to Australia, Affie was shot in the back by Henry James O'Farrell, an Irish Republican. Fortunately, the bullet narrowly missed his spine and he made a full recovery. The would-be assassin was arrested at the scene, quickly tried and executed. Affie, meanwhile, attracted much sympathy and publicity as he convalesced. In Sydney, a vote was taken 'to raise a permanent and substantial monument in testimony of the heartfelt gratitude of the community at the recovery of HRH'. Sufficient funds were raised to build the Royal Prince Alfred Hospital.

The Queen, however, remained unmoved and unimpressed. In a letter to Vicky she wrote:

> I am not as proud of Affie as you might think, for he is so conceited himself and at the present moment receives ovations as if he had done something – instead of God's mercy having spared his life.

She was openly critical of Affie in another letter sent to her eldest daughter in August, and once again compared Bertie in an almost favourable light:

> Yes, Affie is a great, great grief – and I may say source of bitter anger for he is not led astray. His conduct is gratuitous! Oh! he is so different to dear Bertie, who is so loving and affectionate, and so anxious to do well, though he is some times imprudent – but that is all.

A few years later she wrote that Affie was 'Not a pleasant inmate in a house and I am always on thorns and *gêne* [discomfort] when he is at dinner.'

After Affie's marriage to the Grand Duchess Maria Alexandrovna of Russia in January 1874, the Queen decided that she was quite taken with her new daughter-in-law, in sharp contrast to her feelings for her son:

> I have formed a high opinion of her; her wonderfully even, cheerful satisfied temper … Everyone must like her. But alas! not one likes him! I fear that will never get better.

Helena

Just two years younger, Helena, usually called 'Lenchen' by her family – the German nickname for Helena was Helenchen – was Affie's favourite sister. Very close to her father, on his death Helena wrote sadly to a friend:

> What we have lost, nothing can ever replace, and our grief is most, most bitter … I adored Papa, I loved him more than anything on earth, his word was a most sacred law, and he was my help and adviser.

When Victoria discovered that her daughter was becoming romantically attached to her father's former librarian Carl Ruland, who had been employed to teach German to

Bertie, the Queen acted quickly. Ruland was dispatched immediately back to Germany in 1863. At the same time Victoria wrote to Vicky:

> A married daughter I must have living with me [Princess Alice, upon whom the Queen had depended, had not long before left the court for married life in Hesse] … I intend (and she wishes it herself) to look out in a year or two (for till nineteen or twenty I don't intend she should marry) for a young, sensible Prince, for Lenchen to marry, who can during my lifetime make my house his principal home. Lenchen is so useful, and her whole character so well adapted to live in the house, that … I could not give her up, without sinking under the weight of my desolation.

Having determined to keep her daughter close by, Victoria approved her marriage to Prince Christian of Schleswig-Holstein. Fifteen years older than Helena, he had no money and so happily agreed to live in the Queen's Windsor court. Princess Alice objected to the match, seeing it for what it was: a cynical ploy on her mother's part to keep Helena at home. Irate, Victoria denounced Alice as 'A mischief maker and untruth teller!' But the match was also politically difficult as Prussia, Denmark and Austria all claimed the duchies of Schleswig and Holstein, and this led to divisions within the royal family.

Helena, however, was pleased with the choice and

the marriage was a happy one. Like her sisters, Helena possessed a quiet resolve and went on to become one of the founders of the British Red Cross. She was always interested in nursing and was an advocate of nurse registration which became law in 1919. She was also appointed the first president of the newly established School of Art Needlework, which later became the Royal School of Needlework. Like her mother, she enjoyed writing, particularly translation.

Louise

Victoria and Albert's fourth daughter, Princess Louise, was beautiful and headstrong. Interested in art and education, her feminist views and desire for independence were always going to bring her into conflict with her equally strong-minded mother. Her family nickname was 'Little Miss Why'.

In 1858, Victoria wrote to Vicky about her ten-year-old sister, saying, 'Louise very naughty and backward, though improved and very pretty, and affectionate.' She was admiring of her daughter's talent for dancing, noting that Louise 'danced the sword dance with more verve and accuracy than any of her sisters'.

Born in March 1848, Louise was almost fourteen when her father died and Victoria plunged her children, and the court, into the deepest mourning. Dances and entertainments were strictly forbidden and there was no question of a coming-out ball for Louise who found the atmosphere stifling. 'The Queen seems not to wish me to leave her,' she commented. And indeed, Victoria even tried to discourage friendships or any relationship that might tempt Louise away, warning, 'Never make friendships. Girl friendships, and intimacies are very bad and often lead to great mischief.'

Louise was determined to be an artist and eventually persuaded her mother to allow her to go to art school and later to study at the National Art Training School in Kensington. In 1868 she joined a group of other young women training as sculptors. The Queen, herself an accomplished artist, worried about life-drawing classes and tried to limit her daughter's attendance by making Louise her unofficial secretary. But Victoria had underestimated her perseverance and talent. Louise was not willing to allow herself to be controlled.

At the age of twenty-one, Louise developed a close relationship with the sculptor Joseph Edgar Boehm, who had been invited to stay at Balmoral to sculpt a bust of Queen Victoria's personal attendant John Brown. Following the Queen's instructions, Brown spied on the pair and this was enough to convince Victoria that Louise needed a husband.

There were many suitors for the vivacious Princess, but Louise rejected all of the European princes in favour of John Campbell, Marquess of Lorne, heir to the 8th

Duke of Argyll. He appeared cultured, well travelled and educated in comparison to the Prussian princes, whom Louise considered humourless. After initial opposition, the Queen gave her consent for the pair to be married. Writing to Vicky, she admitted:

> I must tell you that I have changed my opinion of Lord Lorne since I have got to know him … and I think him very pleasing, amiable, clever – his voice being only a little against him. And he is in fact very good looking.

Louise married Lord Lorne on 21 March 1871, but their marriage was childless and the couple drifted apart amid rumours of Louise's affairs and Lorne's homosexuality.

The Princess continued to publicly support the arts, higher education and female equality, another area in which she clashed with her mother, who made her own views on the subject of women's suffrage very clear:

> The Queen is most anxious to enlist everyone who can speak or write to join in checking this mad, wicked folly of Women's Rights with all its attendant horrors on which her poor, feeble sex is bent, forgetting every sense of womanly feeling and propriety.

Louise did not dare go as far as to sign a petition in favour of votes for women, but she continued to support women's rights and helped other women to find work and independence. Like Vicky and Alice in Germany, she also worked in hospitals with wounded soldiers.

Louise's marble sculpture of her mother in her coronation robes, which she designed in 1893, still stands outside Kensington Palace to this day.

Arthur

'This child is dear, dearer than the rest put together,' wrote Victoria to her husband. 'Thus, after you he is the dearest, most precious object to me on earth.' Prince Arthur was their seventh child and third son, born in May 1850.

Writing to Vicky in 1858, Victoria remarked of her eight-year-old, 'Arthur is a precious love. Really the best child I ever saw.'

Educated by private tutors and despite never being a great scholar, nor particularly well behaved in lessons, Arthur could do no wrong in his mother's eyes. Victoria was extremely careful to keep him well away from his two older brothers and their bad influence.

Arthur was always fascinated by the army and entered the Royal Military Academy in Woolwich when he was sixteen. On graduation he was commissioned as a lieutenant and went on to serve for forty years in the British Army. He rose to the rank of field marshal and served as Commander of the Third Army Corps and

Inspector-General of the Forces. In 1911, he was appointed the tenth Governor General of Canada.

Arthur continued to please his mother and, writing in 1876, she paid him the highest compliment:

> I have excellent accounts of Arthur. He is so universally respected and liked. He is called 'the model prince' for his wonderfully steady and perfect conduct. He at least follows in his beloved father's footsteps as regards character and sense of duty.

Victoria was less than thrilled by the engagement of her favourite son to Princess Louise Margaret of Prussia, however, and confessed her feelings to her private secretary Henry Ponsonby:

> The Queen cannot deny that she does not rejoice so much at the event – she thinks that so few marriages are really happy now and they are such a lottery. Besides Arthur is so dear a son to her that she dreads any alteration.
>
> But it is entirely his own doing and as she, the Princess, is so much praised and said to be so good, unassuming and unspoilt, serious minded and very English we must hope for the best and that one so good as he is being very happy.

The couple would marry at St George's Chapel, Windsor Castle, in March 1879 and have three children.

Leopold

Following the birth of her fourth son in April 1853, Queen Victoria wrote a letter to her dearest Uncle Leopold:

> Stockmar will have told you that Leopold is to be the name of our fourth young gentleman. It is a mark of love and affection which I hope you will not disapprove. It is a name which is the dearest to me after Albert, and one which recalls the almost only happy days of my sad childhood; to hear 'Prince Leopold' again, will make me think of all those days!

Unfortunately, it soon became obvious that Leopold was a sickly child. At the age of six he was diagnosed with haemophilia, which he had inherited from his mother, and was also believed to suffer with mild epilepsy. After one of Leopold's bad bouts of bleeding, the Queen wrote to Vicky:

> But oh! the illness of a good child is so far less trying than the sinfulness of one's sons – like your two elder brothers. Oh! Then one feels that death in purity is so far preferable to life in sin and degradation!

In 1858, Victoria commented on Leopold's progress in a letter to her eldest daughter:

As for Leopold he still bruises as much as ever, but has not had accidents of late. He is tall, but holds himself worse than ever, and is a very common looking child, very plain in face, clever but an oddity – and not an engaging child though amusing.

Poor child. In comparison with his brothers Leopold was bright and intelligent, but this just seemed to emphasize his physical failings as far as his mother was concerned: 'His mind and head are far the most like of any of the boys to his dear father.' But at various points Victoria referred to him as 'the ugliest and least pleasing of the whole family', and complained about him to Vicky:

He walks shockingly – and is dreadfully awkward – holds himself as badly as ever and his manners are despairing, as well as his speech – which is quite dreadful. It is so provoking as he learns so well and reads quite fluently.

Despite his physical frailty, Leopold was determined and feisty, though in his mother's mind he became a rather saintly, suffering figure after his haemophilia was confirmed.

Leopold was abroad convalescing when his father died in 1861 and when Victoria wrote to him she concentrated on her own misery rather than attempting to comfort her eight-year-old son:

> Poor Mama is more wretched, more miserable than
> any being in this world can be. I pine and long for your
> dearly beloved Papa dreadfully.

On his return to England, Leopold entered a court in mourning, which in effect became a prison for him. He played the piano well and the poet Alfred, Lord Tennyson commented that the Prince 'was considered to be a young man of a very thoughtful mind, high aims, and quite remarkable acquirements.'

Victoria, meanwhile, had other views:

> All the essentially English notions of manliness must be
> put out of the question. He must be constantly watched.
> I do not wish that any attempts should be made to
> remove him from me.

Instead, she appointed Archie Brown, the younger brother of her trusted servant John Brown, to watch over her son. Unfortunately for Leopold, Archie Brown seems to have been a bully, as the Prince was to complain:

> He is fearfully insolent to me, hitting me in the face
> with spoons for fun. He does nothing but jeer and be
> impertinent every day. I could tear him limb from limb I
> loathe him so.

The Queen would not listen to either her son or the

other members of her household who tried to intervene. Leopold wrote even more desperately:

> The life here is becoming daily more odious and intolerable. Every inch of liberty is taken away from one and one is watched and everything one says or does is reported. Oh, how I do wish I could escape from this detestable house. I am looking forward to the day when I can burst the bars of my iron cage and flee away for ever.

When Leopold announced that he wanted to go to university at Oxford, Victoria employed the same tactics she later tried with Beatrice and refused to speak to her son for months. His resolve held and finally, grudgingly, she gave in:

> The inconvenience that it will entail on me of not having a grown up child in the house will be considerable. I have consented on the condition that it is merely for study and that it is not for amusement that you go there.

Far be it for Leopold to have some fun while he was at university, but at least he had escaped to Christ Church, Oxford, even if it meant living with especially selected minders. He greatly enjoyed the relative freedom, study and ideas that he found there. He also met the Liddell family and became good friends with both Edith and her sister Alice, the inspiration for Lewis Carroll's *Alice in Wonderland* and *Alice Through the Looking Glass.*.

After Oxford, Leopold travelled in Europe and through Canada and the United States with his sister Louise and her husband, the Marquess of Lorne, who was then Governor General of Canada. But although Leopold had been made a Privy Councillor and had applied for vice-regal positions in both Australia and Canada, Victoria absolutely refused to appoint him and saw his desire to move away as a personal attack:

> His first duty is to me. But this he has never understood, sad and suffering as I am, I was made quite ill by this new and totally unexpected shock.

Thwarted in every attempt to find a role for himself, Leopold saw marriage as the best option for escaping his mother. Again, the Queen had very decided views on suitable brides for a royal prince, blocking several potential partners. She finally suggested a meeting with Princess Helen of Waldeck and Pyrmont in Germany and the couple would eventually marry at St George's Chapel, Windsor on 27 April 1882. At the wedding ceremony, Victoria disapproved of Leopold using a walking stick, which he had needed after slipping a few weeks before on a visit to Menton in southern France with his mother and younger sister Beatrice. Victoria recorded her thoughts on Leopold's marriage in her journal:

> This exciting day is all over, and past, like a dream, and the last, but one, of my children is married, and has left

the paternal home, but not entirely, as he still keeps his rooms. It was very trying to see the dear boy, on this important day of his life, still lame and shaky, but I am thankful it is well over. I feel so much for dear Helen, but she showed unmistakably how devoted she is to him.

The couple would have two children: Alice in February 1883 and Charles Edward in July 1884.

On 21 February 1884, Victoria noted in her journal:

Leopold started for Cannes to stay at the Villa Nevada there, as he thinks he requires a little change and warmth, but he is going alone, as Helen's health does not allow her to travel just now. I think it rather a pity that he should leave her.

The following month, while convalescing in Cannes, Leopold fell at the yacht club, bumping his knee and head. The accident resulted in severe internal bleeding and in the early hours of 28 March the thirty-year-old Prince died of a brain haemorrhage, four months before the birth of his second child.

Victoria mourned her son and her journal entry for 28 March records her abject sorrow:

Another awful blow has fallen upon me and all of us to-day. My beloved Leopold, that bright, clever son, who had so many times recovered from such fearful illnesses, and from various small accidents, has been take from us! To lose another dear child, far from me [Princess Alice had died six years earlier], and one who was so gifted, and such a help to me, is too dreadful!

Am utterly crushed. How dear he was to me, how I had watched over him! Oh! what grief, and that poor loving young wife …

The poor dear boy's life had been a very tried one, from early childhood! He was such a dear charming companion, so entirely the 'Child of the House' … I am a poor desolate old woman, and my cup of sorrow overflows! Oh! God, in His mercy, spare my other dear children!

Beatrice

The youngest of Victoria and Albert's children, Beatrice was born in April 1857, when her eldest sister Vicky was preparing for marriage and a move to Prussia. Perhaps as a result, the young Princess was showered with attention. The Queen even liked Beatrice as a baby, describing her as a 'pretty, plump and flourishing child … with fine large blue eyes, pretty little mouth and very fine skin'.

When her daughter was three, Victoria wrote: 'Beatrice is my darling, but she is fast, alas! growing out of the baby – is becoming long-legged and thin. She is however still most amusing and very dear.'

After the death of Victoria's mother in March 1861, Victoria wrote to her Uncle Leopold about her youngest child:

> On Sunday our dear little Beatrice was four years old. It upset me much, for she was the idol of that beloved Grandmamma, and the child so fond of her. She continually speaks of her – how she 'is in Heaven', but hopes she will return! She is a most darling, engaging child.

Not yet five when her father died, Beatrice was called 'Baby' by the Queen, who increasingly came to rely on her comforting presence. She wanted to keep Beatrice close by always and for a long time refused to even consider the idea of her fifth daughter marrying.

In April 1863, Victoria wrote to Vicky, making her feelings very clear:

> Many, many thanks for your dear letter of the 14th and for your good wishes for our dear little darling Baby! She is the only thing I feel keeps me alive, for she alone wants me really. She, perhaps as well as poor Lenchen, are the only two who still love me the most of any thing – for all the others have other objects … I know how you all love me, but I see and feel with my terribly sensitive feelings that constantly I am *de trop* to the married children and that every thing I love I must give up!

In October 1873, the Queen was even more pointed:

> … as she [Beatrice] is my constant companion and I
> hope and trust will never leave me while I live, I do not
> intend she should ever go out as her sisters did (which
> was a mistake) but let her see … as much as she can
> with me.

Victoria described Beatrice as having 'the sweetest temper' and said, 'I never saw so amiable, gentle, and thoroughly contented a child as she is'.

Following on from her sisters, Alice, Helena and Louise, Beatrice became her mother's unofficial secretary, helping, as they had done, with political correspondence, as well as other duties. In summer 1871, when Victoria became seriously ill with an abscess on her arm that left her unable to write for a time, she became even more reliant on Beatrice and began dictating her journal to her daughter.

When it became clear to Victoria that Beatrice had developed an affection for a German prince, the Queen placed her next to him at a dinner but ordered her daughter not to speak to him. At the age of twenty-seven, Beatrice announced that she wanted to marry Henry, Prince of Battenberg, to whom she had been introduced at the wedding of her cousin Victoria (daughter of her sister Alice) and Henry's brother Louis. The Queen absolutely refused to speak to Beatrice for seven months, communicating solely by notes pushed across the table. She eventually relented and allowed the marriage to go ahead, but only on the condition that Beatrice and Henry remained living at Windsor and that her daughter continue to work as her secretary.

Victoria wrote to Vicky when matrimonial matters had been settled:.

> I am surprised at myself – considering the horror and dislike of the most violent kind I had for the idea of my precious Baby's marrying at all … how I should have been so much reconciled to it now that it is settled. But it is really Liko [Henry] himself who has so completely won my heart. He is so modest, so full of consideration for me and so is she, and both are quietly and really sensibly happy. There is no kissing, etc. (which Beatrice dislikes) … But the wedding day is like a great trial and I hope and pray there may be no results! That would aggravate everything and besides make me terribly anxious.

After her mother's death Beatrice transcribed and edited the Queen's journals. In line with Victoria's wishes, she took out many of the more private passages to make them suitable for publication. However, she cut so much material that the edited versions are only a third as long as the originals which she eventually burned, though King George V and Queen Mary tried to stop her.

Although Beatrice did not know it, a typed version of the earlier diaries was made by Lord Esher with Bertie's authorization.

Queen and Empress

Queen and Empress

W hen Victoria acceded to the throne she was a young girl of eighteen. She was still just twenty when she married Albert. He became her constant companion and advisor throughout her most formative years as Queen and, in many ways, helped to mould the monarch she became.

The age to which she gave her name was one of huge change and innovation as Britain emerged as a leading industrial nation. She was the first British sovereign to have electricity installed in her home and one of the first people to have a telephone, after Alexander Graham Bell gave the first-ever public demonstration of his invention to the Queen at Osborne House on 14 January 1878.

A constitutional monarch, Victoria nevertheless exerted a great deal of influence. Balanced and often surprisingly liberal in outlook, her political sway is sometimes underestimated and as her confidence grew, she expressed her views openly. Shortly before the Crimean War began in 1853, she wrote to the Prime Minister, Lord Aberdeen, urging:

The Government should take a firm, bold line. This delay – this uncertainty, by which, abroad, we are losing our prestige and our position, while Russia is advancing and will be before Constantinople in no time! Then the Government will be fearfully blamed and the Queen so humiliated that she thinks she would abdicate at once.

Meeting the Public

Never particularly at ease at public ceremonies, Victoria liked nothing more than to travel around the British Isles with her dearest Albert. They both liked the anonymity and freedom that the more remote areas of the country offered them.

In 1846, the Queen and the Prince decided it was time for the young Bertie, as the Duke of Cornwall, to visit his Duchy. While there, husband and wife were both very keen to go down a mine, as Victoria revealed in a diary entry:

It is an iron mine, and one enters on the level. Albert and I got into one of the trucks and were dragged in by miners, Mr. Taylor being so good as to walk behind us. The miners wear a curious dress of wool with a cap, like on the accompanying sketch. They generally have a candle stuck in front of the caps. This time candles were fixed along the inside of the mine, and those of the miners who did not drag or push us, carried lights. There was no room for anyone to pass between the truck and the rock and only just room enough to hold up one's head and even that not always. The whole thing had a most weird effect with the lights at intervals. We got out of the truck and scrambled a little way to see the veins of ore and Albert knocked off some pieces, but usually it is blown off with gunpowder, being so hard. The miners seemed so pleased and are intelligent good people. It was so dazzling when we came up again into the daylight.

'An Humble Cot'

As a young child, Victoria had regularly stayed at Claremont, her Uncle Leopold's country house near Esher in Surrey. Knowing her fondness for the place, Leopold often lent his beloved niece and her husband his residence. After the 1848 revolution in France, the Queen returned the favour, welcoming Leopold's parents-in-law the exiled King Louis Philippe and Queen Marie-Amelie of France, who then stayed in the house. The Queen would buy the property for her youngest son Prince Leopold on his marriage in 1882.

Staying there with their young family in 1842, Victoria and Albert were walking on nearby Oxshott Heath when they were caught in a rainstorm and took shelter in a cottage shed. The Queen wrote about the incident in her journal:

> An old man, who was working in the garden, begged us to walk into the cottage, which we accordingly did, and went into the kitchen, he insisting on our sitting down near the fire. The kitchen was clean and tidy, though he was greatly distressed at its being so dusty. He said it was 'an humble Cot'; he was very civil, poor man, but did not in the least know who we were. He told us his whole history, and that he had been 50 years with the Earl of Fingall.

North of the border, the royal couple increasingly valued their time in the Highlands for the relative freedom it afforded them, as well as the opportunities to meet ordinary people. Victoria's journal entry for 26 September 1857 describes one of many encounters:

> Albert went out with Alfred for the day, and I walked out with the two girls and Lady Churchill, stopped at the shop and made some purchases for poor people and others … [Mrs. Farquharson] walked round with us to some of the cottages to show me where the poor people lived, and to tell them who I was. Before we went into any we met an old woman, who, Mrs. Farquharson said, was very poor, eighty-eight years old,

and mother to the former distiller. I gave her a warm petticoat, and the tears rolled down her old cheeks, and she shook my hands, and prayed God to bless me: it was very touching.

The Queen made her first railway journey on 13 June 1842, no doubt encouraged by her husband. Prince Albert, ever interested in industry and science, had already travelled by rail on several occasions, the first on 14 November 1839 when he went from Slough to Paddington station in London after visiting his future wife at Windsor Castle. The couple would make that same journey in 1842. The Great Western Railway company ran the line and had just two days' notice of the royal visit. Victoria and Albert's carriage was specially adapted and two extra carriages were positioned between their own and the engine for added safety, as railway accidents at the time were not unusual. The royal party travelled in a horse-drawn carriage from Windsor Castle to Slough station. Their train left promptly at midday and arrived at Paddington twenty-five minutes later, having kept to a suitably stately speed.

The Queen wholeheartedly approved:

We arrived here [Buckingham Palace] yesterday morning, having come by the railroad, from Windsor, in half an hour, free from dust and crowd and heat, and I am quite charmed with it.

Foreign Affairs

In April 1865, Queen Victoria was most alarmed by news of the assassination of Abraham Lincoln, the President of the United States. She wrote to her Uncle Leopold, 'I only hope it will not be catching elsewhere.'

She had some reason to be concerned, as during her reign she was the target of at least seven assassination attempts and even had a stalker. Edward Jones, known as 'the Boy Jones', broke into Buckingham Palace several times between 1838 and 1841, sitting on her throne, hiding beneath furniture and allegedly stealing her underwear.

Victoria felt great sympathy for the President's widow, understanding the grief she would be feeling all too well. Although she had never met either Lincoln or the First Lady, the Queen was moved to write to Mary Todd Lincoln:

> Though a stranger to you, I cannot remain silent when so terrible a calamity has fallen upon you and your country, and must express personally my deep and heartfelt sympathy with you under the shocking circumstances of your present dreadful misfortune.
>
> No one can better appreciate than I can, who am myself utterly broken-hearted by the loss of my own beloved husband, who was the light of my life, my stay, my all, what your sufferings must be; and I earnestly

pray that you may be supported by Him to Whom alone the sorely stricken can look for comfort, in this hour of heavy affliction!

In 1864, Prussia and Austria had defeated Denmark to take control of Schleswig and Holstein. The resulting struggle for supremacy in Germany was to lead to the Austro-Prussian war two years later. Her daughter Vicky may have been Crown Princess of Prussia, courtesy of her marriage, but that did not stop Victoria expressing her dislike of the kingdom, as she wrote in August 1865:

In Germany things look rather critical and threatening. Prussia seems inclined to behave as atrociously as possible, and as she always has done! Odious people the Prussians are, that I must say.

Emperor and Friend

The state visit of Napoleon III and the Empress Eugénie in April 1855 began as an official duty, with both couples feeling anxious about the meeting, as there had been enmity between Britain and France for centuries. However, relations soon relaxed into a friendship. The emperor was very short and Victoria thought him odd looking, 'with a head and bust, which ought to belong to a much taller man'. Nevertheless, she discovered that they 'got on extremely well ... and my agitation soon and easily went off'.

Writing about the visit of the French dignitaries to her uncle, she remarked:

> The impression is very favourable. There is great fascination in the quiet, frank manner of the Emperor, and she is very pleasing, very graceful, and very unaffected, but very delicate. She is certainly very pretty and very uncommon-looking. The Emperor spoke very amiably of you.

In May 1855, the Queen wrote a memorandum reflecting on Napoleon III's character:

> That he is a very extraordinary man, with great qualities there can be no doubt – I might almost say a mysterious man. He is evidently possessed of indomitable courage, unflinching firmness of purpose, self-reliance, perseverance, and great secrecy; to this should be added, a great reliance on what he calls his Star, and a belief in omens and incidents as connected with his future destiny, which is almost romantic – and at the same time he is endowed with wonderful self-control, great calmness, even gentleness, and with a power of fascination, the effect of which upon all those who become more intimately acquainted with him is most sensibly felt.

This first meeting was followed by a state visit to Paris in August 1855. Victoria came to value Eugénie's friendship and the two developed a close bond. She wrote enthusiastically about the trip to her Uncle Leopold later that month:

> I am delighted, enchanted, amused, interested, and think I never saw anything more beautiful and gay than Paris – or more splendid than all the Palaces. Our reception is most gratifying …
>
> The Emperor has done wonders for Paris, and for the Bois de Boulogne … The heat is very great, but the weather splendid, and though the sun may be hotter, the air is certainly lighter than ours – and I have no headache …
>
> The children are so fond of the Emperor, who is so very kind to them. He is very fascinating, with that great quiet and gentleness. He has certainly excellent manners, and both he and the dear and very charming Empress (whom Albert likes particularly) do the *honneurs* extremely well and very gracefully, and are full of every kind attention.

In her journal, the Queen continued her summation: 'Altogether I am delighted to see how much my Albert likes and admires her [Eugénie], as it is so seldom I see him do so with any woman.' She referred to Eugénie, Albert and Napoleon discussing at length, 'Principalities, – difficulties, – rapprochements, alliance, etc.'

For her part, Victoria was always full of praise for Eugénie's appearance and dress sense, often remarking that 'she looked very pretty, and was in very good spirits' or describing how she was 'lovely in simple white embroidered cambric dress with lilac ribbons' and 'lovely in a light organdie dress, embroidered all over with violets, a wreath to match, in her hair, and pearls'.

There is occasionally a sense that at times Victoria might have preferred to leave the business of politics to Albert and instead concentrate on being a wife and mother. She expressed something of this in a letter to her Uncle Leopold:

> Albert becomes really a terrible man of business. I think it takes a little off from the gentleness of his character, and makes him so preoccupied. I grieve over all this, as I cannot enjoy these things, much as I interest myself in general European politics; but I am every day more convinced that we women, if we are to be good women, feminine and amiable, and domestic, are not fitted to reign; at least it is *contre gré* [against one's will] that they drive themselves to the work which it entails.

When the Third Republic was declared in France in 1870 following the defeat of Napoleon III's army during the Franco-Prussian War, Napoleon and Eugénie sought refuge in England. They settled in Camden Place, in Chislehurst, Kent. Victoria visited them there and continued to receive her friends at court.

The Queen Alone

The loss of her husband and adviser in 1861 had left Victoria feeling isolated and lonely. For a time, even dinners with her extended family and in-laws were beyond her, and state duties nothing but a burden.

'Felt so nervous, all being in state and I alone!' she wrote in her journal, and to her Uncle Leopold, who had been encouraging her to return to work more than a year after Albert's death, she explained her difficult situation:

> You say that work does me good, but the contrary is the fact with me, as I have to do it alone, and my Doctors are constantly urging upon me rest. My work and my worries are so totally different to any one else's: ordinary mechanical work may be good for people in great distress, but not constant anxiety, responsibility and interruptions of every kind, where at every turn the heart is crushed and the wound is probed! I feel too visibly how much less able for work I am than I was.

Empress of India

India, its people, languages and food had long held a special place in the Queen's imagination and interest. She was fascinated by the country and was also sympathetic to it, although she never visited. During the Mutiny of 1857, Victoria read about 'dreadful details in the papers of the horrors committed in India' and was increasingly appalled at the reports:

> Oh! When I think and talk of my own sorrows … and reflect on the fearful appalling horrors which have taken place in India, and on the hundreds of families who have lost sons – Husbands – brothers – and what is so infinitely worse had daughters – sisters – wives – and friends murdered, butchered, tortured – with a refinement of fiendish atrocity which one couldn't believe … how unbearably small does every suffering of ours appear!

The Queen had remarkably open-minded views on race in comparison with the more widely held prejudices of the day. She defended Charles Canning, the Governor-General of India, who had been given the nickname 'Clemency' on account of his liberal views and support for more humane measures.

Victoria wrote that she shared Canning's 'feelings of sorrow and indignation at the unchristian spirit shown – alas! also to a great extent here – by the public towards Indians in general and towards Sepoys without discrimination!' She felt strongly 'that there is no hatred to a brown skin'.

In October 1875 Bertie left England on a tour of India. He had sought Benjamin Disraeli's backing for the visit and there is no doubt that her Prime Minister's approval had persuaded the Queen to allow the trip, although she immediately began to question how fit for the task her son really was and also to object to his all-male travelling companions:

> I am trying all I can to get some better and more eminent persons added to this list … but the difficulty is very great and I fear dear B. has a number of *soi-disant* [so-called] friends who put all sorts of ideas into his head.

Despite Victoria's reservations, the visit was a huge success. The Prince of Wales enjoyed meeting people and taking part in the pomp and ceremony that a royal tour entailed. He was very well received and, like his mother, expressed quite enlightened views for the times: 'Because a man has a black face and a different religion from our own, there is no reason why he should be treated as a brute.'

As much as she admired the country, though, Victoria was bored by her son's letters home which described his travels in great detail:

> Bertie's progresses lose a little interest and are very wearing – as there is such a constant repetition of elephants – trappings – jewels – illuminations and fireworks.

There is more than a hint that the Queen was jealous of Bertie's popularity and success. It would only be a matter of time before her eldest daughter Vicky became Empress of Germany (on the death of her elderly father-in-law, Emperor Wilhelm I) and so Disraeli suggested that the time was right for Victoria to accept the title of Empress of India. The matter was raised in part to flatter Her Majesty, but also because it chimed with the mood of the general population.

Unlike his Whig rival, William Gladstone – of whom the Queen once complained, 'He speaks to Me as if I was a public meeting' – Disraeli was very much a favourite of Victoria. The colourful statesman is quoted as stating, 'Everyone likes flattery and when you come to royalty you should lay it on with a trowel.'

He got on well with the Queen and also knew when to appeal to her vanity. For instance, after the publication of her book *Leaves from the Journal of Our Life in the Highlands from 1848 to 1861*, Disraeli would confidentially say to her, 'We authors, Ma'am'. The book was first printed in January 1868 and immediately sold 20,000 copies. It was translated into several languages and all royalties from the sales were donated to charity. She presented a copy of the book to the author Charles Dickens with the dedication, 'From the humblest of writers to one of the greatest.'

The Royal Titles Bill, which was drafted to recognize Victoria as Empress of India, was presented to Parliament in early 1876 by Prime Minister Disraeli. Much to the Queen's dismay, it caused considerable controversy. The Whigs in opposition denounced it as an attempt to introduce 'bastard imperialism' into the British monarchy. In March that same year she wrote to Theodore Martin, whom she had commissioned to write *The Life of the Prince Consort*:

> The reason the Queen now writes to Mr. Martin is to ask whether he cannot get inserted into some papers a small paragraph to this effect, only worded by himself: 'There seems a very strange misapprehension on the part of some people, which is producing a mischievous effect; viz. that there is to be an alteration in the Queen's and Royal family's ordinary appellation. Now this is utterly false. The Queen will be always called "the Queen", and her children "their Royal Highnesses", and no difference whatever is to be made except officially adding after Queen of Great Britain, "Empress of India", the name which is best understood in the East, but which Great Britain (which is an Empire) never has acknowledged to be higher than Queen or King.'

Despite the initial dispute, the Royal Titles Act was finally passed by parliament and Victoria took the title 'Empress of India' from 1 May 1876.

Incidentally, Bertie only found out about the change in his mother's title courtesy of the press and was furious that he had not been informed directly. The Queen generally tried to exclude the Prince of Wales from all state business, continuing to doubt his abilities. When particularly vexed, she even went so far as to say, 'I often pray he may never survive me for I know not what would happen.'

When Bertie returned home from his four-month visit to India, it was to a rapturous welcome from the public. As Victoria informed Vicky in her letter of 16 May 1876:

> Bertie's arrival and the hearty reception he met with and
> I also met with, which was very striking and of which
> I sent you an account … was a proof of the immense
> loyalty of the country.

Two days later, in response to a reply from her daughter, the Queen wrote again but this time seemed rather put out: 'You speak only of the enthusiasm for Bertie! That for your own Mama was I thought much greater.'

Munshi Abdul Karim

Queen Victoria was a skilled linguist. Fluent in English and German, she also spoke French, Italian and Latin, and was interested in other languages that were less widely known in Victorian Britain. Later in life she began learning Hindustani from Abdul Karim, one of her Indian servants. The Queen noted in her journal:

> I am learning a few words of Hindustani to speak to my servants. It is a great interest to me for both the language and the people, I have naturally never come into real contact with before.

Karim had been appointed to the Royal Household along with Mohammed Buksch in 1887, the year of the Queen's Golden Jubilee. He was eventually promoted to the role of the Queen's Indian Secretary.

Victoria described both men in her journal entry for 23 June 1887:

> The one, Mohamed Buxsh [sic], very dark with a very smiling expression … and the other, much younger, called Abdul Karim, is much lighter, tall, and with a fine serious countenance. His father is a native doctor at Agra.

She wrote in praise of their services to her private secretary Henry Ponsonby:

> Abdul is most handy in helping when she signs by drying her signatures. He learns with extraordinary assiduity and Mahomet is wonderfully quick and intelligent and understands everything.

An entry in the Queen's journal for August 1888 explains her decision to promote Abdul Karim:

> Am making arrangements to appoint Abdul a *munshi*, as I think it was a mistake to bring him over as a servant to wait at table, a thing he had never done, having been a clerk or *munshi* in his own country and being of rather a different class to the others. I had made this change, as he was anxious to return to India, not feeling happy under the existing circumstances. On the other hand, I particularly wish to retain his services, as he helps me in studying Hindustani, which interests me very much, and he is very intelligent and useful.

Later that same year she wrote:

> Had my last Hindustani lesson, as good Abdul goes home to India to-morrow on leave, which I regret, as it will be very difficult to study alone, and he is very handy and useful in many ways.

Munshi Abdul Karim remained at the Queen's service for the last fifteen years of her reign, much to the disapproval of other members of her Household who objected to his pretensions and felt he was wholly unqualified for the position of Queen's Indian Secretary. Naturally Victoria refused to listen. She continued to take him with her when travelling and kept up her language lessons.

Victorian Values

Queen Victoria was always fond of dogs and had several pets, from her Cavalier King Charles Spaniel Dash, who was her girlhood companion and with her when she became Queen, to her favourite Pomeranian Turi, who lay beside her on her deathbed. She once commented, 'Nothing will turn a man's home into a castle more quickly and effectively than a dachshund.' Victoria also had an African Grey parrot called Coco that could sing the National Anthem. She liked animals of all kinds and strongly disapproved of cruelty towards them.

In 1868, the Queen wrote to the Home Secretary Gathorne Hardy, asking him to make enquiries about the treatment of animals in society:

Nothing brutalises people more than cruelty to dumb animals, and to dogs, who are the companions of man, it is especially revolting.

The Queen is sorry to say, that she thinks the English are inclined to be more cruel to animals than some other civilised nations are.

Animals were also a feature of her letters to Vicky:

How are all your dogs? I feel so much for animals – poor, confiding, faithful, kind things and do all I can to prevent cruelty to them which is one of the worst signs of wickedness in human nature!

After one of Vicky's cats had been shot and cruelly mutilated in August 1980, her mother was completely sympathetic:

Let me say how horrified and how distressed I am about your cat! … I would cry with you as I adore my pets … I think it right and only due to the affection of dumb animals, who (the very intelligent and highly developed ones) I believe to have souls, to mourn for them truly and deeply.

Victoria loved music and the theatre. Writing enthusiastically in her journal about the opera singer Giulia Grisi's portrayal of Desdemona in Rossini's *Otello* in 1834, she wrote: 'I was very much amused indeed!' In fact her very own pencil drawing of the singer in character is in the Royal Collection.

It was the young Victoria's love of opera that encouraged her to learn Italian. After listening to Handel's *Messiah* in York Minster in 1835, the Princess reviewed the performance and revealed her musical preferences:

I must say with the exception of a few Choruses and one or two songs it is very heavy and tiresome … I am not at all fond of Handel's music, I like the present Italian school such as Rossini, Bellini, Donizetti etc., much better.

Prince Albert shared his wife's profound interest in music. He was a gifted pianist and had also composed several pieces. The couple enjoyed playing piano and singing together. Among the music performed at Bertie and Alix's wedding ceremony on 10 March 1863 was one of Albert's very own compositions. Victoria noted in her journal that 'Dearest Albert's Chorale was sung, which affected me much, and the service proceeded.'

The soprano Jenny Lind also sang a solo during the service. Albert and Victoria had been very impressed by the Swedish opera singer. Lind was often called the 'Swedish Nightingale' and was also a close associate of Felix Mendelssohn. After one of her performances the Queen wrote:

> The great event of the evening was Jenny Lind's appearance and her complete triumph. She has a most exquisite, powerful and really quite peculiar voice, so round, soft and flexible and her acting is charming and touching and very natural.

Victoria was a talented watercolourist. Since childhood, she had always illustrated her journals with drawings and watercolour sketches, and as an adult she took drawing lessons with the artist, illustrator and nonsense poet Edward Lear.

From an artistic perspective both Victoria and Albert appreciated male physical beauty. They drew and painted the naked male form, although Victoria worked from photographs rather than life models, and the couple also had a growing collection of erotic art.

Writing to Vicky in 1859 about their shared interest in art, Victoria questioned her daughter on her choice of materials:

I hear you model and even paint in oils; this last I am sorry for; you remember what Papa always told you on the subject. Amateurs never can paint in oils like artists and what can one do with all one's productions? Whereas water colours always are nice and pleasant to keep in books or portfolios. I hope, dear, you will not take to the one and neglect the other!

⊱☙ Nearest and Dearest ☙⊰

H.M. KING LEOPOLD I. IN 1863

Nearest and Dearest

Queen Victoria has been described as emotional, obstinate, honest and straight-talking, so it is no surprise that she held strong opinions on friends and relations, developing passionate attachments to those she loved and equally strong dislikes for those who displeased her.

Victoria's Relationship with her Mother

As a child, the young Princess Victoria was very isolated. Growing up in Kensington Palace with her widowed mother, Victoria Duchess of Kent, her every move was governed by the 'Kensington System'. This exacting set of rules had been devised by the Duchess and her close adviser, Sir John Conroy, and controlled every aspect of the Princess's upbringing. It restricted Victoria's meetings with other children or members of the family, and ensured her absolute dependence upon her mother and Conroy. The Duchess was very protective of her daughter as heir to the throne, but Conroy's motives were more political. He assumed the Duchess would be appointed regent when the young Princess became Queen and that he in turn would become private secretary and adviser to both, giving him a great deal of personal influence and power.

Victoria detested Conroy, the Kensington System and her complete lack of freedom. She was never alone, was forced to sleep in her mother's room and was not even allowed to go downstairs unless someone was there to hold her hand. Bread-and-milk suppers were not uncommon and she had a sharp brooch tied under her chin to ensure she kept her head up while eating.

Later in life, Victoria wrote about her childhood memories:

> I had led a very unhappy life as a child – had no scope
> for my very violent feelings of affection … and did not
> know what a happy domestic life was.

Becoming Queen liberated Victoria and offered her a power she had never before experienced. Of her coronation on 28 June 1838, Victoria wrote in her journal: 'I shall ever remember this day as the proudest of my life.'

She moved to Buckingham Palace largely to escape the suffocating control of her mother and where she relegated the Duchess to an apartment far away from her own. She also set about banishing her arch-nemesis Sir John Conroy, but this was not difficult as he was generally unpopular at court. Lord Melbourne himself was moved to remark, 'My God! I don't like this man. There seems to be something odd about him.'

Conroy was quickly excluded from the Queen's Household. One of Victoria's first acts was to dismiss Sir John, although he remained in her mother's service for several years. Lord Melbourne negotiated the pension and settlement.

The first years of Victoria's reign saw a coolness develop between the new Queen and her mother, which was not helped by the Duchess's continued reliance upon and friendship with Conroy, and her reluctance to stop trying to influence her daughter. In August 1837, Victoria wrote to her mother in frustrated tones:

> I thought you would not expect me to invite Sir John Conroy after his conduct towards me for some years past … I imagined you would have been amply satisfied with what I had done for Sir John Conroy, by giving him a pension of £3,000 a year, which only Ministers receive, and by making him a Baronet …

In her journal of 15 January 1838, she writes simply, 'Got such a letter from Mama, oh! oh! such a letter.' In another entry she records that she told Lord Melbourne, 'How dreadful it was to have the prospect of torment for many years by Mama's living here.'

Mother and daughter were finally reconciled after the birth of Victoria's first child in 1840, probably influenced by Albert. By this time, Conroy was no longer working for the Duchess and lived abroad. Relations were also helped once Baroness Lehzen had been dismissed at Albert's insistence, as the former governess had not approved of either the Duchess or of Conroy.

In May 1859, one of the royal doctors, Sir James Clark, warned Prince Albert that the Duchess of Kent was suffering from a type of cancer which would eventually prove fatal. The Duchess spent most of the month unwell, often in bed. Then, the day after Victoria's fortieth birthday on 25 May, a telegram arrived with news that her mother was weak and not eating. In the event, she recovered and gained strength, but the Duchess was almost seventy-three and Victoria suddenly realized that she would not always be there. She wrote of this worry to her Uncle Leopold:

I am thoroughly shaken and upset by this awful shock; for it came on so suddenly – that is came like

a thunderbolt upon us, and I think I never suffered as
I did those four dreadful hours till we heard she was
better! I hardly myself knew how I loved her, or how
my whole existence seems bound up with her – till
I saw looming in the distance the fearful possibility
of what I will not mention. She was actually packing
up to start for here! [Victoria, Albert and the rest of
the family, including Vicky visiting from Prussia, were
gathered together at Osborne House to celebrate the
Queen's birthday.] How I missed her yesterday I cannot
say, or how gloomy my poor birthday on first getting
up appeared I cannot say. However, that is passed –
and please God we shall see her, with care, restored to
her usual health ere long.

Almost two years later, the Duchess was again taken ill.
After an operation to treat an abscess on her arm, she
at first seemed to be recovering. But on 15 March 1861
Victoria realized that there was little hope, writing in her
journal of her sadness:

Oh, what agony what despair was this. I knelt before
her, kissed her dear hand and placed it next my cheek;
but though she opened her eyes, she did not, I think,
know me. She brushed my hand off, and the dreadful
reality was before me, that for the first time she did not

know the child she had ever received with such tender smiles! I went out to sob.

The Queen was with her mother at Frogmore House, in the grounds of Home Park, Windsor, when she died on 16 March 1861. One of her first letters was to her mother's brother, Uncle Leopold:

On this, the most dreadful day of my life, does your poor broken-hearted child write one line of love and devotion. She is gone! That precious, dearly beloved tender Mother – whom I never was parted from but for a few months – without whom I can't imagine life – has been taken from us! It is too dreadful! But she is at peace – at rest – her fearful sufferings at an end! It was quite painless – though there was very distressing, heartrending breathing to witness. I held her dear, dear hand in mine to the very last, which I am truly thankful for! ... Dearest Albert is dreadfully overcome – and well he may, for she adored him!

Ten days later, Victoria wrote to her uncle once again:

On Sunday I took leave of those dearly beloved remains – I had never been near a coffin before, but dreadful and heartrending as it was, it was so beautifully arranged that it would have pleased her, and most probably she looked down and blessed us – as we poor mortals knelt around, overwhelmed with grief! ...

But oh! dearest Uncle – the loss – the truth of it – which I cannot, do not realize even when I go (as I do daily) to Frogmore – the blank becomes daily worse!

The constant intercourse of forty-one years cannot cease without the total want of power of real enjoyment of anything. A sort of cloud which hangs over you, and seems to oppress everything … Long conversation, loud talking, the talking of many people together, I can't bear yet …

I try to be, and very often am, quite resigned – but dearest Uncle, this is a life sorrow. On all festive or mournful occasions, on all family events, her love and sympathy will be so fearfully wanting. Then again, except Albert (who I very often don't see but very little in the day), I have no human being except our children, and that is not the same … and besides, a woman requires a woman's society and sympathy sometimes, as men do men's … My poor birthday, I can hardly think of it! Strange it is how often little trifles, insignificant in themselves, upset one more even than greater things.

On 30 March, Victoria wrote to her Uncle Leopold from Buckingham Palace:

It is a comfort for me to write to you, and I think you may like to hear from your poor motherless child. It is to-day a fortnight already, and it seems but yesterday …

We have an immense deal to do – and everything is in the greatest order, but to open her drawers and presses, and to look at all her dear jewels and trinkets in order to identify everything, and relieve her really excellent servants from all responsibility and anxiety, is like a sacrilege, and I feel as if my heart was being torn asunder! So many recollections of my childhood are brought back to me …

Frogmore we mean to keep just as dear Mamma left it – and keep it cheerful and pretty as it still is. I go there constantly; I feel so accustomed to go down the hill, and so attracted to it, for I fancy she must be there …

Albert is so kind, and does all with such tenderness and feeling.

Shortly afterwards, the royal family left for the 'air and quiet' of Osborne on the Isle of Wight. From there, on 9 April, Victoria sent another letter to her uncle:

It is touching to find how she treasured up every little flower, every bit of hair. I found … touching relics of my poor Father, in a little writing-desk of his I had never seen, with his last letters to her, and her notes after his death written in a little book, expressing such longing to be reunited to him! Now she is! … All these notes show how very, very much she and my beloved Father loved each other … Then her love for me – it is too touching! I have found little books with the accounts of my babyhood, and they show such unbounded tenderness! Oh! I am so wretched to think how, for a time, two people [Sir John Conroy and Baroness Lehzen] most wickedly estranged us! ... To miss a mother's friendship – not to be able to have her to confide in – when a girl most needs it, was fearful! I dare not think of it – it drives me wild now! But thank God! that is all passed long, long ago, and she had forgotten it, and only thought of the last very happy years.

And all that was brought by my good angel, dearest Albert, who she adored, and in whom she had such unbounded confidence.

After her mother died, Victoria was grief-stricken. With his wife unable to cope with her public role, Albert took on an increasing number of her duties, wearing himself out and damaging his already fragile health.

Dearest Sister

As a child, Victoria was very close to her elder half-sister Feodora, despite an age gap of more than eleven years. Before Victoria's widowed mother married her second husband Prince Edward, Duke of Kent and Strathearn, as Princess Victoria of Saxe-Coburg-Saalfeld she had first married Emich Carl, Second Prince of Leiningen. and had two children: Carl was born in 1804 and became the Third Prince of Leiningen; Feodora was born in 1807.

Victoria and Feodora were brought up together in Kensington Palace, where both were privately tutored, until Feodora married in 1828 and moved away to live at Schloss Langenburg in Leiningen, Germany. From then onwards, the sisters wrote regularly to one another and both looked forward to Feodora's visits to England.

In June 1834, Feodora arrived with her husband Ernest I, Prince of Hohenlohe-Langenburg, and their two eldest children. It was the first time that the sisters had seen one another in six years. Victoria wrote, 'Dear Feodora looks very well but is grown much stouter since I saw her.'

When Feodora left on 28 July, Victoria's journal reflects their sadness at parting:

> The separation was indeed dreadful. I clasped her in my arms and kissed her and cried as if my heart would break; so did she, dearest Sister. We then tore ourselves from each other in the deepest grief … When I came home I was in such a state of grief that I knew not what to do with myself. I sobbed and cried most violently the whole morning … My dearest best sister was friend, sister, companion all to me, we agreed so well together in all our feelings and amusements … I love no one better than her.

On Victoria's accession, Feodora wrote to her with words of encouragement: 'Living but for your duty to your country, difficult as it is, will prove to you a source of happiness.'

A letter for Victoria dated 1854 that was found among Feodora's papers stated:

I can never thank you enough for all you have done for me, for your great love and tender affection. These feelings cannot die, they must and will live in my soul – till we meet again, never more to be separated – and you will not forget.

Victoria last saw her sister early in 1872 during a visit to Baden-Baden in Germany, when Feodora was already seriously ill. After her death later that same year, the Queen committed her thoughts to her journal on 23 September:

Can I write it? My own darling, only sister, my dear excellent, noble Feodora is no more! … I stand so alone now, no near and dear one near my own age, or older to whom I could look up to, left! All, all gone! She was my last near relative on an equality with me, the last link with my childhood and youth. My dear children, so kind and affectionate, but no one can really help me.

Dearest Best Lehzen

Although Victoria later blamed her governess for causing friction with her mother, Louise Lehzen had exerted a great deal of positive influence on the young Princess. She remained a close confidante throughout Victoria's youth and the early years of her reign.

Writing about her childhood in 1872, Victoria remembered:

> At five years old, Miss Lehzen was placed about me, and though she was most kind, she was very firm and I had a proper respect for her. I was naturally very passionate, but always most contrite afterwards. I was taught from the first to beg my maid's pardon for any naughtiness or rudeness towards her.

When sixteen-year-old Victoria was taken ill while staying in Ramsgate, it was her governess who looked after her. Her journal entry for 5 November 1835 stated:

> Dear good Lehzen takes such care of me and is so unceasing in her attentions to me that I shall never be able to repay her sufficiently for it but by my love and gratitude. I never can sufficiently repay her for all she has borne and done for me. She is the most affectionate, devoted, attached and disinterested friend I have and I love her most dearly.

She later added: 'My dearest best Lehzen has been and still is (for I require a great deal of care still) most unceasing and indefatigable in her great care of Me.'

At her coronation three years later, she revealed that 'It was my dearly beloved angelic Lehzen, whose eyes I caught when on the Throne, and we exchanged smiles.'

When Baroness Lehzen died in 1870, Victoria remembered the companion of her youth with the greatest affection:

My dearest kindest friend, dear old Lehzen, expired quite quietly and peacefully on the 9th. For two years she had been quite bedridden, from the results of breaking her hip. Though latterly her mind had not been clear, still there were days when she constantly spoke of me, whom she had known from the age of six months. She had devoted her life to me, from my fifth to my eighteenth year, with the most wonderful self-abnegation, never even taking one day's leave! After I came to the throne she got to be rather trying and especially so after my marriage, but never from any evil intention, only from a mistaken idea of duty and affection for me. She was an admirable governess, and I adored her, though I also feared her.

A Faithful Highlander

John Brown served both Victoria and Albert at Balmoral where he accompanied them on expeditions and was a part of their daily life there. He had been employed as a young man before the royal couple bought the estate. One of the first mentions of the faithful Highland servant who was to mean so much to the Queen after her beloved Albert's death is in her journal entry of 4 September 1860, when he accompanied them on a tour with Lady Churchill and General Grey.

> Breakfasted at Balmoral in our own room at half-past seven o'clock, and started at eight or a little past, with Lady Churchill and General Grey, in the sociable (Grant and Brown on the box as usual) for Castleton where we changed horses … We had decided to call ourselves Lord and Lady Churchill and party, Lady Churchill passing as Miss Spencer, and General Grey as Dr. Grey! Brown once forgot this and called me 'Your Majesty' as I was getting into the carriage; and Grant on the box once called Albert 'Your Royal Highness;' which set us off laughing, but no one observed it.

In October 1861, before Albert's last illness and death, Victoria praised Brown's services in a letter to her Uncle Leopold:

> We have had a most beautiful week … I going out every day about twelve or half-past, taking luncheon with us, carried in a basket on the back of a Highlander, and served by an invaluable Highland servant I have, who is my factotum here, and takes

the most wonderful care of me, combining the offices
of groom, footman, page, and maid, I might also
say, as he is so handy about cloaks and shawls, etc.
He always leads my pony, and always attends me out
of doors, and such a good, handy, faithful, attached
servant I have nowhere; it is quite a sorrow for me to
leave him behind.

After Albert died, Victoria retreated from London life and
spent an increasing amount of time in Scotland, often in
the company of her trusted servant:

Lord Aberdeen was quite touched when I told him I
was so attached to the dear, dear Highlands and missed
the fine hills so much. There is a great peculiarity about
the Highlands and Highlanders; and they are such a
chivalrous, fine, active people.

During the early years of mourning, Balmoral, where
Victoria could sketch, ride and take the air, was a place of
comfort. It was Princess Alice who first noticed that one
of the few times her grieving mother appeared almost
happy was when driving out in the pony cart led by John
Brown and it was she who suggested that Brown should
accompany the Queen to Osborne in December 1864.

In February 1865, the Queen informed her Uncle
Leopold by letter that 'I continue to ride daily ... on my
pony, and have now appointed that excellent Highland

servant of mine to attend me always and everywhere out of doors, whether riding or driving or on foot.'

The following month she told Vicky about a diplomatic reception at Buckingham Palace – 'a great bore' – with hundreds attending, including the Prussian Ambassador and his wife:

> The good Bernstorffs were, as usual, in a sort of porcupine condition which is so odious. It seems to me such a loss of time to be always offended and Brown's observation about a cross person seems to me very applicable here 'it can't be very pleasant for a person themselves to be always cross' which I think so true and so original. His observations upon everything he sees and hears here are excellent and many show how superior in feeling, sense and judgment he is to the servants here! The talking and indiscretion shocks him.

From that time, John Brown became Victoria's constant companion, wherever she was. He brought her private correspondence and took her riding. Brown made the Queen laugh and she liked his humour. A heavy drinker himself, he also brought her whisky, his motto being, 'Don't stay thirsty.'

However, his bluff manners and arrogance soon brought the Highlander into conflict with other members of the Household, including her private secretaries

Charles Grey and Henry Ponsonby. Brown was also a source of irritation to members of Victoria's family. But as with all those of whom the Queen was fond throughout her life, Victoria could see no fault with her trusted servant. She clarified the situation in a letter to Vicky, dated April 1865:

I have not, I think, told you that I have taken good J. Brown entirely and permanently as my personal servant for out of doors – besides cleaning my things and doing odd 'jobs' – as I found it so convenient and saving me so much trouble to have one and the same person always for going out, and to give my orders to, which are taken by him from me personally to the stables. He comes to my room after breakfast and luncheon to get his orders – and everything is always right; he is so quiet, has such an excellent head and memory, and is besides so devoted, and attached and clever and so wonderfully able to interpret one's wishes. He is a real treasure to me now.

The Queen had long before admitted to her sister-in-law Princess Alexandrine, the wife of Albert's brother Ernest, that 'servants are often the best friends to have.'

To her Uncle Leopold, Victoria wrote in February 1865: 'It is a real comfort, for [Brown] is devoted to me – so simple, so intelligent, so unlike an ordinary servant, and so cheerful and attentive.'

Writing to Vicky, she explained that, 'I feel I have here and always in the House a good devoted Soul … whose only object and interest is my service, and God knows how much I want so to be taken care of.'

The Queen's reliance upon John Brown had not gone unnoticed. Politicians and courtiers would barely hide their smirks as she praised her servant's good qualities, and satirical pamphlets were circulating freely, referring to the monarch as Mrs Brown. There was also a spoof version of her *Leaves from the Journal of Our Life in the Highlands* called *John Brown's Legs, or Leaves from a Journal in the Lowlands*. Bertie had complained that despite being her son and the Prince of Wales he was barely mentioned in his mother's book, while Brown appeared throughout. Other members of the family had similarly disapproved. However, Victoria remained blissfully unaware of the gossip and rumours. She continued to defend Brown to her sons and daughters who were growing increasingly hostile.

On 29 March 1883, the Queen's journal noted some heartbreaking news:

Leopold came to my dressing-room and broke the dreadful news to me that my good, faithful Brown had passed away early this morning. Am terribly upset by this loss, which removes one who was so devoted and attached to my service and who did so much for my personal comfort. It is the loss not only of a servant, but of a real friend.

There is no doubt how deeply she felt Brown's death. A few days later she wrote to her private secretary Henry Ponsonby:

> The Queen is trying hard to occupy herself but she is utterly crushed and her life has again sustained one of those shocks like in 1861 when every link has been shaken and torn and at every turn and every moment the loss of the strong arm and wise advice, warm heart and cheery original way of saying things and the sympathy in any large and small circumstances – is most cruelly missed.

Writing to Vicky about her recent bereavement she revealed:

> The terrible blow which has fallen so unexpectedly on me – and has crushed me – by tearing away from me not only the most devoted, faithful, intelligent and confidential servant and attendant who lived and, I may say (as he overworked himself) died for me – but my dearest best friend has so shaken me … The shock – the blow, the blank, the constant missing at every turn of the one strong, powerful reliable arm and head almost stunned me and I am truly overwhelmed. The sympathy is universal – the appreciation of his noble, grand and yet simple nature – true and great – which is soothing.

And in another letter to her daughter, she went on to explain:

> I am crushed by the violence of this unexpected blow which was such a shock – the reopening of old wounds and the infliction of a new very deep one. There is no rebound left to recover from it and the one who since 1864 had helped to cheer me, to smooth, ease and facilitate everything for my daily comfort and who was my dearest best friend to whom I could speak quite openly is not here to help me out of it! I feel so stunned and bewildered and this anguish that comes over me like a wave every now and then through the day or at night is terrible! He protected me so, was so powerful and strong – that I felt so safe! And now all, all is gone in this world and all seems unhinged again in thousands of ways!

After visiting her faithful servant's grave at Crathie, near Balmoral, in August 1883, Victoria wrote in her journal:

> Went in the pony chair to the Kirkyard where I visited good Brown's grave and looked at the granite stone I have had placed over it which is simple and nice, and I laid a wreath there. It always upsets and makes me sad to realise that that excellent and faithful servant is really gone, never to return.

Following John Brown's death, Victoria wanted to publish a third volume of her Highland journals, which were in reality a memoir of Brown. It took all the efforts and diplomacy of Randall Davidson, the Dean of Windsor, and Henry Ponsonby to dissuade the Queen from doing so. She regarded any snide comments as 'ill-natured gossip in the higher classes' and was utterly convinced that Brown was a popular figure. She remained set on publication before finally letting the matter drop. According to one of Ponsonby's sons, the manuscript was later destroyed.

Victoria had left very detailed instructions about her burial and, as well as various family rings and photographs, she requested that a lock of John Brown's hair, his mother's wedding ring (which she wore on the third finger of her right hand) and some photographs of him, together with several of his letters, were all included in her coffin. The statues and private memorials to Brown made by Victoria were later destroyed by Bertie, who had often clashed with the trusted Highlander and particularly resented his influence over the Queen. Bertie also had the life-size statue of Brown by Edgar Boehm that his mother had commissioned, moved to a more out of the way site at Balmoral.

The Queen
in Mourning

The Queen in Mourning

Prince Albert's personal workload had been exhausting. As well as his own projects, he managed the royal estates and finances and assisted his wife in most of her public duties. He drafted her correspondence and was also present when she met with ministers. In May 1860 he compared himself to a donkey on a treadmill, saying, 'He, too, would rather munch thistles in the castle moat. Small are the thanks he gets for his labour.'

By the age of forty, Albert was not a well man. He was suffering from severe stomach cramps, as well as frequent headaches, insomnia, toothache and various other aches and pains. Victoria was not overly sympathetic. After her own nine pregnancies and labours, she tended to find Albert's physical weaknesses rather trying.

The death of her mother on 16 March 1861 had left the Queen shocked and despairing. At the time Victoria described it to her Uncle Leopold as 'the most dreadful day of my life.' With his wife grieving and unable to cope, Albert undertook even more of her day-to-day responsibilities.

In November that year, Albert received word that gossip was circulating in the gentlemen's clubs and foreign press that his eldest son Bertie had been having an affair with an actress named Nellie Clifden. Nineteen-year-old Bertie's brief and inappropriate liaison with the woman had shocked and horrified both his parents, but Albert in particular was consumed by anxiety over the matter. He saw it as a threat to the stability and moral standing of the monarchy and at night he was unable to sleep, pacing the floors with worry.

On 25 November, Albert travelled to Cambridge to see his son. Walking in the rain through the city's streets, the pair talked for hours. Worn out, cold and wet, afterwards Albert was wracked with pain. Over the next few days his symptoms worsened. On 9 December, the Prince's doctor William Jenner diagnosed typhoid fever, but the gastric problems that had plagued Albert for the last two years of his life suggest there was an underlying health issue such as Crohn's disease, renal failure or even cancer.

Victoria was hopeful of a good recovery initially, but in mid-December Bertie was called home. Albert died on 14 December at Windsor Castle. His wife and five of their children were at his bedside.

Dear Uncle Leopold

Throughout Albert's last illness, Victoria wrote frequently to her Uncle Leopold. The first letter was written on 26 November, the day after Albert's visit to Bertie in Cambridge:

My beloved Uncle … Albert is a little rheumatic, which is a plague – but it is very difficult not to have something or other of this kind in this season, with these rapid changes of temperature; *unberufen*, *unberufen*, [touch wood] he is much better this winter than he was the preceding years.

On 4 December she sent Leopold an update:

My dearest Uncle – I have many excuses to make for not writing yesterday, but I had a good deal to do, as my poor dear Albert's rheumatism has turned out to be a regular influenza, which has pulled and lowered him very much. Since Monday he has been confined to his room. It affects his appetite and sleep, which is very disagreeable, and you know he is always so depressed when anything is the matter with him. However, he is decidedly better to-day, and I hope in two or three days he will be quite himself again. It is extremely vexatious, as he was so particularly well till he caught these colds, which came upon worries of various kinds.

And two days later, Victoria wrote of the prospect of Albert's recovery:

My beloved Uncle – I am thankful to report decidedly better of my beloved Albert. He has had much more sleep, and has taken much more nourishment since yesterday evening. Altogether, this nasty, feverish sort of influenza and deranged stomach is on the mend, but it will be slow and tedious, and though there has not been one alarming symptom, there has been such restlessness, such sleeplessness, and such (till to-day) total refusal of all food, that it made one very, very anxious, and I can't describe the anxiety I have gone through! I feel to-day a good deal shaken, for for four nights I got only two or three hours' sleep. We have, however, every reason to hope the recovery, though it may be somewhat tedious, will not be very slow. You shall hear again to-morrow. Ever your devoted Niece.

Victoria's journal entry for 7 December, however, reflected the depths of her despair:

I went to my room and cried dreadfully and felt oh! as if my heart must break – oh! such agony as exceeded all my grief this year. Oh, God! Help and protect him! … I seem to live in a dreadful dream. My Angel lay on the bed in the bedroom and I sat by him watching him and the tears fell fast.

To her daughter Vicky, the Queen wrote:

Dearest Papa is going on as favourably as we could wish … But it is all like a bad dream! To see him prostrate and worn and weak, and unable to do any thing and never smiling hardly – is terrible.

I am well but very tired and nervous for I am so constantly on my legs – in and out and near him. I sleep in my dressing-room, having given up our bedroom to dear Papa.

Her journal entry of 9 December describes her increasing worry:

He wanders frequently and they say it is of no consequence tho' very distressing, for it is unlike my own Angel. He was so kind calling me 'gutes Weibchen' [excellent little wife], and liking me to hold his dear hand. Oh! it is an anxious, anxious, time but God will help us thro' it.

On 11 December Victoria wrote to Leopold once again from Windsor Castle:

Dearest Uncle – I can report another good night, and no loss of strength, and continued satisfactory symptoms. But more we dare not expect for some days; not losing ground is a gain, now, of every day.

It is very sad and trying for me, but I am well, and I think really very courageous; for it is the first time that I ever witnessed anything of this kind though I suffered from the same at Ramsgate, and was much worse. The

trial in every way is so very trying, for I have lost my
guide, my support, my all, for a time – as we can't ask
or tell him anything. Many thanks for your kind letter
received yesterday. We have been and are reading Von
Ense's book to Albert; but it is not worth much. He likes
very much being read to as it soothes him. W. Scott is
also read to him.

The next day, her letter to her uncle was again hopeful:

My beloved Uncle – I can again report favourably of
our most precious invalid. He maintains his ground
well – had another very good night – takes plenty
of nourishment, and shows surprising strength. I am
constantly in and out of his room, but since the first four
dreadful nights, last week, before they had declared it
to be gastric fever – I do not sit up with him at night as I
could be of no use; and there is nothing to cause alarm.
I go out twice a day for about an hour. It is a very trying
time, for a fever with its despondency, weakness, and
occasional and invariable wandering, is most painful
to witness – but we have never had one unfavourable
symptom; to-morrow, reckoning from the 22nd, when
dear Albert first fell ill – after going on a wet day to
look at some buildings [the Prince had also inspected
new buildings at Sandhurst in the rain and was already
complaining of rheumatic pains when he made the
journey to see Bertie on 25 November] – having likewise

been unusually depressed with worries of different kinds – is the end of the third week; we may hope for improvement after that, but the Doctors say they should not be at all disappointed if this did not take place till the end of the fourth week. I cannot sufficiently praise the skill, attention, and devotion of Dr. Jenner, who is the first fever Doctor in Europe, one may say … Albert sleeps a good deal in the day. He is moved every day into the next room on a sofa which is made up as a bed. He has only kept his bed entirely since Monday. Many, many thanks for your dear, kind letter of the 11th. I knew how you would feel for and think of me. I am very wonderfully supported, and, excepting on three occasions, have borne up very well.

Albert's Death

By 13 December, the doctors thought all was going well and Dr Watson assured the Queen that he had 'seen many infinitely worse cases … and … I never despair with fever'. Prince Albert was being given brandy every half-hour to avoid congestion on the lungs and there seemed grounds for hope. He was moved into the Blue Room at Windsor Castle, not altogether auspiciously as both King William IV and King George IV had died there, but early on the morning of 14 December Dr Brown was optimistic that the crisis was over.

Victoria's journal for 1861 ends on 13 December. It was not until February 1872, over ten years later, that she could bring herself to describe the events of her beloved husband's final day:

> Went over at 7 as I usually did. It was a bright morning; the sun just rising … Never can I forget how beautiful my darling looked lying there with his face lit up by the rising sun, his eyes unusually bright …

The Queen walked on the Terrace with Princess Alice. In the distance she heard the military band playing and began to cry. By the afternoon, Albert's face had a 'dusky hue'. The doctors suggested the children should be brought to see their father. Victoria went to lie down in the next room but hearing a change in Albert's breathing she hurried back to his bedside:

> But the breathing was the alarming thing – so rapid, I think 60 respirations a minute … I bent over him and said to him '*Es ist Kleines Frauchen*' [it is your little wife] and he bowed his head; I asked him if he would give me '*ein Kuss*' [a kiss] and he did so. He seemed half dozing, quite quiet … Alice was on the other side, Bertie and Lenchen … kneeling at the foot of the bed … Two or three long, but perfectly gentle breaths were drawn, the hands clasping mine and (oh! It turns me sick to write it) all, all, was over … I stood up, kissed his dear heavenly

forehead and called out in a bitter agonizing cry, 'Oh! my dear Darling!' and then dropped on my knees in mute, distracted despair, unable to utter a word or shed a tear.

Albert's Treasurer, Colonel Charles Beaumont Phipps, carried the distraught Queen to a sofa and Bertie ran across to hug his mother, assuring her, 'Indeed, Mama, I will be all I can to you.' She kissed her son and said, 'I am sure, my dear boy, you will.'

Vicky, hearing the sad news in Germany, wrote, 'Why has the earth not swallowed me up? To be separated from you at this moment is a torture which I can not describe.'

On the same day Victoria began a letter to Vicky with the words 'My darling Angel's child – Our firstborn. God's will be done.' The letter continued:

What is to become of us all? Of the unhappy country, of Europe, of all? For you all, the loss of such a father is totally irreparable! I will do all I can to follow out all his wishes – to live for you all and for my duties. But how I, who leant on him for all and everything – without whom I did nothing, moved not a finger, arranged not a print or photograph, didn't put on a gown or bonnet if he didn't approve it shall be able to go on, to live, to move, to help myself in difficult moments? How I shall long to ask his advice! Oh! it is too weary! The day – the night (above all the night) is too sad and weary. The days never pass! I try to feel and think that I am living on with him, and that his pure and perfect spirit is guiding and leading me and inspiring me!

… I long so to cling to and clasp a loving being. Oh! how I admired Papa! How in love I was with him! How everything about him was beautiful and precious in my eyes! Oh! how, how I miss all, all!

It was not until 20 December that Victoria wrote to her Uncle Leopold from Osborne House to inform him of Albert's death:

My own dearest, kindest Father – For as such have I ever loved you! The poor fatherless baby of eight months is now the utterly broken-hearted and crushed widow of forty-two! My life as a happy one is ended! the world is gone for me! If I must live on (and I will do nothing to make me worse than I am), it is henceforth for our poor fatherless children – for my unhappy country, which has lost all in losing him – and in only doing what I know and feel he would wish, for he is near me – his spirit will guide and inspire me! But oh! to be cut off in the prime of life – to see our pure, happy, quiet, domestic life, which alone enabled me to bear my much disliked position, cut off at forty-two – when I had hoped with such instinctive certainty that God never would part us, and would let us grow old together (though he always talked of the shortness of life) – is too awful, too cruel!

And yet it must be for his good, his happiness! His purity was too great, his aspiration too high for this poor, miserable world! His great soul is now only enjoying that for which it was worthy! And I will not envy him – only pray that mine may be perfected by it and fit to be with him eternally, for which blessed moment I earnestly long. Dearest, dearest Uncle, how kind of you to come! It will be an unspeakable comfort, and you can do much to tell people to do what they ought to do. As for my own good, personal servants – poor Phipps in particular – nothing can be more devoted, heartbroken as they are, and anxious only to live as he wished!

Good Alice has been and is wonderful.

Albert's premature death left his wife utterly bereft. Victoria was lost in her sorrow, withdrawing from public appearances and wearing black as a sign of mourning for the rest of her life. Her reluctance to go to London led to her being nicknamed the 'Widow of Windsor'.

Writing in January 1862, a few weeks after Albert's death, the Queen revealed:

I have been unable to write my journal since the day my beloved one left us, and with what a heavy broken heart I enter on a new year without him! … My dreadful and overwhelming calamity gives me so much to do,

that I must henceforth merely keep notes of my sad
and solitary life. This day last year found us so perfectly
happy, and now!! Last year music woke us; little gifts,
new year's wishes, brought in by maid, and then given
to dearest Albert, the children waiting with their gifts
in the next room – all these recollections were pouring
in on my mind in an overpowering manner … Felt as if
living in a dreadful dream.

Albert's significance to Victoria was summed up
poignantly in a letter she wrote to Vicky:

He was my father, my protector, my guide and adviser
in all and everything. My mother, I might say, as well as
my husband. I suppose no one ever was so completely
altered and changed in every way as I was by dearest
Papa's blessed influence.

In October 1862, Victoria travelled to Saxe-Coburg and
from there sent a letter to her Prime Minister Lord
Palmerston about her feelings on revisiting Albert's
childhood home:

The Queen's nerves and strength and general health are
just the same, and everything approaching to society
or even having several of her own family together with

her at her meals, is more than she can bear. But, trying and heartrending in many ways she found going to dear Coburg was, the many dear recollections of her beloved Angel's childhood and youth (as well as of her dear mother), seeing the many scenes (so beautiful and peaceful in themselves), he so loved and the many kind old attached friends, high and low, – the hearing his native tongue – and the breathing of his native air – were soothing and sweet in their very sadness to her bruised spirit and her aching, bleeding heart!!

On the first anniversary of Albert's death, Dr Stanley, who later became Dean of Westminster, led a service of prayers and remembrance for the Queen and family in Albert's room at Windsor, which Victoria described in her journal:

Oh! this dreadful, dreadful day! At 10 we went into the dear room (all the children but Baby there) … the room was full of flowers, and the sun shining in so brightly, emblems of his happiness and glory, which comforted me. I said it seemed like a birthday, and Dr. Stanley answered, 'It is a birthday in a new world.' Oh! to think of my beginning another year alone!

Two years later, his loss was still as raw and she continued to feel life without him was unbearable: 'Here I sit lonely and desolate, who so need love and tenderness.' Looking back, and perhaps remembering some of her temper tantrums in response to anything approaching criticism from her husband, she commented, 'Dear Darling. I fear I tried him sadly.'

In December 1865 she wrote in her journal:

I cannot believe I am writing for the third time on this terrible anniversary. It seems but yesterday and there again so far off … Went in [to Albert's Mausoleum] to pray and gaze at that peaceful and beautiful face of the statue. What a day of harrowing memories.

She gave short shrift to the senior cleric who dared to suggest that the widowed Queen should now consider herself as 'married to Christ', snapping, 'That's what I call twaddle!'

'This dreadful anniversary, the 10th returned again.' In December 1871 Bertie was seriously ill with typhoid fever and the Queen had been fearful: 'Instead of this date dawning on another deathbed, which I had felt almost certain of, it brought the cheering news that dear Bertie had slept quietly …' Fortunately, the Prince of Wales went on to make a full recovery.

In mid-December 1878 – 'This terrible day come round

again' – sad news came from Germany that Princess Alice had died from diphtheria. Victoria wrote, 'Went, as I always do on this day, to the Blue Room [where Albert had died], and prayed there.'

In 1895, the Queen remarked on 'this terrible anniversary returned for the thirty-fourth time':

When I went to my dressing-room found telegrams saying that dear May [her granddaughter-in-law Mary of Teck] had been safely delivered of a son at three this morning. Georgie's [later King George V] first feeling was regret that this dear child should be born on such a sad day. I have a feeling it may be a blessing for the dear little boy, and may be looked upon as a gift from God!

The baby was to become King George VI, father of Queen Elizabeth II.

On the anniversary of Albert's death in 1899, Victoria wrote in her journal:

Already thirty-eight years since that dreadful catastrophe which crushed and changed my life, and deprived me of my guardian angel, the best of husbands and most noble of men!

Queen Victoria mourned Albert for forty years, and every day had her servants lay out hot water and a set of clothes for him until her own death in 1901. She kept a marble model of 'his sweet little ear' close by her, and his rooms in all their homes were unchanged, even the glass from which he drank his last sip of medicine remained, unmoved, on his bedside table.

On state occasions such as her Golden Jubilee service on 21 June 1887, she remained acutely aware of his loss:

> This very eventful day has come and is passed … [at the service in Westminster Abbey] I sat alone (oh! without my beloved husband, for whom this would have been such a proud day!) … The Te Deum, by my darling Albert, sounded beautiful.

To Lord Rosebery, her Prime Minister, she confessed:

> Alone I did feel, in the midst of so many, for I could not but miss sadly those who were so near and dear, and who would have so rejoiced in those rejoicings, above all him to whom the nation and I owe so much!

At the Queen's funeral in February 1901, her coffin contained many mementoes of family, friends and servants, and included one of Albert's dressing gowns and a plaster cast of his hand. She was buried beside her dearest beloved angel in the huge granite tomb inside the Royal Mausoleum at Frogmore within Home Park, Windsor Castle.

Bibliography

The Letters of Queen Victoria, A Selection From Her Majesty's Correspondence Between the Years 1837 and 1861, Volume 1 1837-1843, Volume 2 1844-1853, Volume 3 1854-1861, by Queen of Great Britain Victoria

Duff, David, ed., *Queen Victoria's Highland Journal*, Webb & Bower, 1980

Esher, Reginald Baliol Brett, *The Girlhood of Queen Victoria, A Selection from Her Majesty's Diaries Between the Years 1832 and 1840, In Two Volumes*, Volume 1 1832-1838, Volume 2 September 1838–February1840, John Murray, 1912 and Forgotten Books

Fulford, Roger, *Your Dear Letter: Private Correspondence of Queen Victoria and the Crown Princess of Prussia, 1865-1871*, Evans Bros, 1971

Fulford, Roger, *Darling Child: Private Correspondence of Queen Victoria and the Crown Princess of Prussia, 1871-1878*, Evans Bros, 1976

Fulford, Roger, *Beloved Mama: Private Correspondence of Queen Victoria and the Crown Princess of Prussia, 1878–1885*, Evans Bros, 1981

Gash, Norman, *Aristocracy and People*, Edward Arnold, 1979

Gray, Annie, *The Greedy Queen: Eating With Victoria*, Profile Books, 2017

Hibbert, Christopher, *Queen Victoria: A Personal History*, HarperCollins, 2000

Hibbert, Christopher, *Queen Victoria in her Letters and Journals*, John Murray, 1984 and Sutton Publishing, 2000

Longford, Elizabeth, *Queen Victoria (Essential Biographies)*, The History Press, 2009

Roberts, Andrew, ed., *Letters to Vicky*, Folio Society, 2011

Strachey, Lytton, *Queen Victoria*, Chatto & Windus, 1921

Wilson, A.N., *Victoria A Life*, Atlantic Books, 2014

www.ForgottenBooks.com

www.royal.uk

Queen Victoria's Journals – From 24 May 2012, Queen Victoria's Journals can be accessed online through a partnership between ProQuest, the Royal Archives and the Bodleian Libraries at qvj.chadwyck.com and www. queenvictoriasjournals.org

Picture Credits

Victoria and Albert: A Passionate Partnership
Victoria wedding: ILN

Victoria as Wife and Mother
Victoria, baby, Duke of Wellington: Wellcome Collection CC BY 4.0

Sons and Daughters
Winterhalter family group: from *The Beautiful Life and Illustrious Reign of Queen Victoria* by Rev. John Rusk, Ph.D, Chicago 1901

Queen and Empress
Queen Victoria, enthroned, holding fan: from *Life of Her Most Gracious Majesty, The Queen, Vol. III*, by Sarah Tytler, Toronto 1887

Nearest and Dearest
Leopold I: from *The History of Belgium, Part II 1815 – 1865* by Demetrius C. Boulger, London 1909

The Queen in Mourning
Queen Victoria in black, reading: from *The Personal Life of Queen Victoria* by Sarah A. Tooley, London 1901

About the Author

Karen Dolby has written widely on subjects for adults and children, both fiction and non-fiction. Her previous books range from the history of nursery rhymes and popular songs, to ghost stories, puzzle adventures and memory development.

Her most recent titles for Michael O'Mara Books are: *The Wicked Wit of Queen Elizabeth II*, *The Wicked Wit of Prince Philip* and *The Wicked Wit of Princess Margaret*.

Karen divides her time between south London and France.